# When Canada joined Cape Breton

## Celebrating Fifty Years of the Canso Causeway

## Elaine Ingalls Hogg

foreword by Mary Morrison

NIMBUS
PUBLISHING LTD

Nimbus Publishing Limited
PO Box 9166
Halifax, NS    B3K 5M8
(902) 455-4286

Printed and bound in Canada
Design: Margo Ellen Gesser

Library and Archives Canada Cataloguing in
Publication

    Hogg, Elaine Ingalls
    When Canada joined Cape Breton : celebrating
    50 years of the Canso Causeway / Elaine Hogg.

    ISBN 1-55109-514-9

1. Canso Causeway (N.S.)—History. 2. Cape
Breton Island (N.S.)—History. I. Title.

FC2325.9.C35H63 2005    971.6'904
C2004-905992-0

We acknowledge the financial support of the
Government of Canada through the Book
Publishing Industry Development Program
(BPIDP) and the Canada Council for our publishing
activities.

## PHOTO CREDITS

Bob Martin Studios: 36, 70
Florence Cook: 23
Roger Cyr: 10, 18
Roy Einarson: 4, 8, 12*, 16*, 19*, 22*, 24, 25, 27
  (both), 28, 30, 51 (bottom), 56 (*refinished by
  Bernie MacDonald)
Yvonne Fox: 85
Burchell Fulmore: 13
Cyril Gillis: 91
Mindy Haight: 51 (top)
Shirley Hartery: 88 (left)
A. J. Hatfield: 40
Carol Haverstock: 90
Iris Hayes: 112 (both)
Diane Hayman: 54
Elaine Hogg: 74
Grant MacDaniel, *The Reporter*, Port Hawkesbury:
  100
Cathy MacDonald: 48
Grant MacDonald: 38 (top)
Rachel MacFarlane: 35 (bottom), 79
Thomas MacInnis: 113
Donald MacIntosh: 50
Barbara MacKinnon: 104
Arnold MacLean: 91
Stuart MacLeod, Jr.: 32
Michael MacNeil: 38 (bottom), 41, 43,
Marilyn MacPhee: 98
Rilla McLean: 5, 88 (both, right), 87, 92
Clarence McLennan: 26
Marion Noakes: i, iv, vi, viii, x, 5, 7,
Joyce Oliver: 59 (both)
Donna Paris: 17
Port Hastings Historical Society: 34, 35 (top), 84
  (both), 86, 95, 96
Gilbert van Ryckevorself: 67
Joe Tummonds: 47

*COVER IMAGE: Early picture of the Causeway. Graham
Geddes found this picture of the Causeway among his
grandfather's keepsakes. Captain Arthur Henry Smith, a
veteran of both world wars, was proud of his march across
the causeway during its opening.*

# CONTENTS

*Dedicated to my husband, Hugh, who has been a
great source of support and encouragement.*

The Strait of Canso before the Causeway was built, with winter drift ice blocking the shipping lane.

*"I am a Cape Breton patriot, so it simply reflects my pride of place when I refer to the time
when Canada joined Cape Breton."*

Ian McNeil, "Information Morning," CBC Radio, Sydney, Nova Scotia

# PREFACE

The sight of the Canso Causeway does something to the heart. About three years ago, I was paying my bill at a restaurant in Aulds Cove when I struck up a conversation with one of Cape Breton's well-known Celtic music ambassadors. "I'm on my way home from Ontario," he said with a smile. "Going to do some concerts." As we talked, he told me of leaving his beloved Cape Breton for Ontario to join the priesthood in the fifties. In the next few minutes, he shared memories forever imprinted on his mind: the type of car he was driving, the condition of the gravel road to the causeway, and his impression of the new link to the mainland. He remembered that they drove with the windows down, partly because there was no air conditioning and partly on account of the two small children in the car. "In those days there wasn't any Pampers," he explained with a mischievous twinkle in his eye.

On my way home, I began thinking of my own personal links to the causeway: reading about the grand opening as a child in school, crossing it with my future husband and his parents as a teenager, coming to Cape Breton to find work in the seventies, and the many crossings since then. I knew that many people had similar memories, and I began imagining a kind of history that would draw these stories together. One person who shared my vision was Bernie MacDonald, originally from Mulgrave and now living in Ottawa. "Ah, Elaine, thy name is temptation, thy land is blessed and thy spirit is reminiscence," he wrote, then promptly contributed four stories as well as immeasurable help in rounding up and restoring old photographs. Friend and former neighbour Rilla McLean spent hours sharing her research, giving me leads for interviews and writing articles. Her assistance has been invaluable.

As a collection of stories, the book is far from complete; however, it is my hope that the following pages will inspire others to share their stories for future generations. There are many thousands more people out there—tourists, island residents, travellers to Newfoundland and Labrador, mainlanders—who have their own memories linked to the Causeway, recollections of the time when Canada joined Cape Breton.
—Elaine Ingalls Hogg

Strait of Canso from Port Hawkesbury, N.S.

# FOREWORD

## by Mary Morrison

You know that expression, "making a mountain out of a molehill?"

Well, my husband Gordie referred to the construction of the Canso Causeway as the "making a molehill out of a mountain." "It's not right, I don't like it," he said for the tenth time since we left Gardiner Mines. He was sitting forward in his seat, his chin almost touching the steering wheel as he tried to stay exactly in the centre of his lane. He always drove as though the divider line and the shoulder of the road were dotted with landmines. If he occasionally veered a couple of inches left or right, he jerked the wheel, bringing the car back to the middle. Interesting for the people coming behind us.

It was August 13, 1955, and we were on our way to the official opening of the Canso Causeway. Gordie, who was as stubborn then as he is today, was going to try to stop them from making what he considered to be a colossal mistake. I went along to try to stop him from making a bigger one. He was opposed to having a causeway because he felt that easy access to the Island would be a threat to our

way of life, or so he said. The truth was that a permanent link to the rest of the country would make it easier for his relatives—who, mercifully, had moved away to find a "better life"—to come back. Every measure had to be taken to prevent this from happening.

"Why now?" I asked him. "Why kick up a big stink now? Where were you when they started to build the Causeway?"

"To tell you the truth," he said, "I didn't think they'd go through with it. Who ever heard of building a road out of mountain?"

"Apparently, everyone in the country but you," I answered.

For miles I tried to reason with him. I told him that a hundred-member pipe band was tuned up and ready to play and that once the pipers had gone through the trouble of blowing up the bags, he'd be hard pressed to summon a force powerful enough to stop the tunes from finding the air.

I had time on my side since Gordie is and always has been the slowest driver ever to be issued a license. In hindsight, I realize that I could have saved myself a boatload of worry if

I'd just gone ahead on foot and warned everyone that trouble was coming, even if it was only coming at 15 miles per hour.

We arrived in time to see the pipers marching across the Causeway, kilts swinging as every man and woman who looked on wondered the same thing. Perhaps if the wind picked up we'd all have our answer.

Gordie got out of the car and immediately began searching for an official, someone in charge, someone who could be reasoned with. I watched him disappear into the crowd and hoped that whatever transpired would not leave him with a permanent criminal record.

After a few minutes I went after him. I found him standing at full attention, saluting, tears streaming down his face. I guess it was all too much for him. The tartans, the music and the happy faces of the onlookers had all conspired to distract him from his purpose, which was to embarrass himself and generations of Morrisons to come.

What started out to be a day full of potential disaster turned out to be one of the loveliest days of that or any other summer. On the long, long drive home, Gordie and I talked about the many trips that we would take over the Causeway to places we'd never been before. And we would take those trips whenever his relatives threatened to visit us.

~ *Mary Morrison*

A sailboat on the Strait of Canso.

*Bette MacDonald (Mary Morrison) is a Gemini Award winning actress from Cape Breton who still gets a little rush when she crosses the Causeway to come home.*

# STATISTICS

- Number of railway cars ferried across the Strait of Canso in 1920: **40,000**
- After World War II, the average number of railcars per day to cross the Strait: **311**
- Number of ferry trips in a nineteen-hour day: **17**
- Number of railcars per year: **113, 515**
- Length of Canso Causeway across water: **1310.6 metres (4300 feet)**
- Surface width of Canso Causeway: **24.4 metres (80 feet)**
- Depth of Canso Causeway: **66 metres (218 feet)**
- Amount of rock fill used in Canso Causeway: **9.1 million metric tonnes (10,000,262.7 tons)**

CANAL SPECIFICATIONS:
- Canal and locks: **1202 metres (3,945 feet)**
- Length: **250 metres (820 feet) between gates**
- Width: **24.4 metres (80 feet)**

BRIDGE SPECIFICATIONS:
- Length: **308 metres (94 feet)**
- Weight: **909 tonnes (1000 tons)**
- Pivot of swing-bridge: **96.5 centimetres (38 inches)**
- Average number of vehicles per day to cross the Canso Causeway in 1956: **714**
- Average number of vehicles per day to cross the Canso Causeway in 2002: **8040**
- Average number of boats per year through the Canso Canal in 1956: **1273**
- Average number of boats per year through the Canso Canal in 2002: **2042**

*Point Tupper with a view of the train–ferry dock in the distance.*

# CHAPTER 1

# BEGINNINGS

*"The ferry across the water is just one more great memory of all the happy times experienced in beloved Cape Breton. How do I say thank you? Just a thank you, I guess, but know that my note is filled with love for the land and the people of Cape Breton." ~ Francis E. (Frank) Chisholm*

Cape Breton Island is 175 kilometres long and 140 kilometres wide and it forms the eastern part of the Canadian province of Nova Scotia. For centuries the island has been home to Mi'kmaq. After John Cabot landed on the island in 1497 and claimed it for England, Cape Breton was used as a fur trading and fishing outpost—and later, when it was handed back to Britain in the Treaty of Paris, the island was a prize of war between France and England.

Thousands of Irish and Scottish settlers came to Cape Breton to live in the 1700s and 1800s. The island also became a place of safety for Acadians returning to Nova Scotia after the Expulsion (1755–1762) and a new homeland for the Loyalists displaced by the American Revolution (1775–1783). While pockets of Italian, Polish, Ukrainian, Lebanese, Greek and many other cultures are scattered across the island, the fact that Cape Breton became a refuge for a large number of Scottish immi-

grants after the Battle of Culloden in 1746 has contributed to the strong presence of Scottish culture everywhere in Cape Breton. For generations, men and women, boys and girls have gathered in their kitchens and shared the literature, dances, music and folktales of their homeland.

Because Islanders were separated from the mainland by the Strait of Canso, a narrow strait of fast-running tides, it wasn't long before their isolation sparked discontent. As early as February 1829 a petition in Hugh McMillan's handwriting states: "He [McMillan] therefore trusts that the Honourable House will grant him such a sum of money as in their wisdom they may think fit to as to enable him to keep a comfortable ferry for men and cattle." McMillan, followed by his son Alex and grandson Hugh, was the first of three generations of ferrymen to transport mail and passengers by horse and sleigh across the Strait when it was full of ice. In 1883, sixteen-year-old Mulgrave resident John O'Neil petitioned his neighbours to urge the government to finance a bridge connecting the island to the mainland. Other advocates for a permanent crossing before 1900 included Senator Dave McKeen and John MacDonald, a merchant from Iona. The railway bridge built across Grand Narrows at Iona inspired them. Aside from these private petitions, the change in the island's main industries from fishing and farming to coal-mining and steel-making made a fixed link all the more necessary, as coal and steel needed to be moved from the island to world markets quickly and efficiently.

The first improvement in connecting the island to the rest of the province came in the form of a train and ferry service. Although its first scheduled trip wasn't until June 2, 1892, the Intercolonial Railway (now Canadian National) first linked Cape Breton to the mainland with its run from New Glasgow to Sydney on November 24, 1890. The train crossed the Strait from Mulgrave to Point Tupper on Nova Scotia's pioneer steel ship, a barge-like ferry known as the SS *Mulgrave*. However, high winds, strong currents and winter ice in the Strait soon made it apparent that the ferry was an unsafe method of transport. For example, on February 11, 1938, Robert Francis Martell, son of M. J. and Julie (Petrie) Martell, was born in the "Woodstock" drawing room of a Pullman car during a winter ferry crossing that had been delayed for thirty-five hours due to ice jams in the Strait . On the baby's first birthday, CNR Railway presented the boy with a lifetime pass on its trains.

The SS *Mulgrave* was followed by two other train ferries, the *Scotia I* in 1901 and the *Scotia II* in 1915. Once again, the long delays and unscheduled trips caused by nature blowing the ferries off course gave citizens, business owners and governments cause to imagine a permanent link. They considered a bridge, tunnel, or causeway.

With 90,000 motor vehicles being transported over the Strait by the ferries in 1949 and an average of 113,000 railway cars in the

In the late 1880s two local merchants, E. A. MacNeil and H. F. Mac Dougall (Mac Dougall was also the local Member of Parliament) from Iona, Cape Breton, convinced the owners of Intercolonial Railway to build the railway through the centre of Cape Breton, particularly through the communities of Iona and Grand Narrows. In order to cross the deep water over the Barra Strait, a seven-span iron bridge was built, thus connecting these otherwise isolated communities with Sydney and industrial Cape Breton.

years after the war up to 1950, Cape Bretoners dreamed of being connected to the mainland. In "The Bochan Bridge of Canso," a poet dreams of a bridge and imagines the sights and crossings; *bochan* is the Gaelic word for ghost. Hon. Angus L. MacDonald, Premier of Nova Scotia, often waxed wordy on his favourite topic—a Strait crossing. His brother, Dan, called it a bochan bridge, believing such a feat to be impossible. Local lore attributes this poem to him.

## THE BOCHAN BRIDGE OF CANSO

Oh, do you hear the traffic's whine?
And do you see the lights in line
From MacMillan's Point to Porcupine?
It's the Bochan Bridge of Canso.

It glimmers in the pale moonlight.
And you can see it any night—
Provided you have second sight
The Bochan Bridge of Canso.

There's Angus L. with shears in hand.
Before the crowd he takes his stand.
Then snips the glimmering moonlight band
On the Bochan Bridge of Canso.

Then Rod MacLean comes prancing o'er
And shakes the bridge from shore to shore.
And loud is heard his thundering roar
On the Bochan Bridge of Canso.

MacKinnon and MacIvor came
Followed by the halt and lame—
At the election it's the same
On the Bochan Bridge of Canso.

A thousand foremen stood about
The old machine gave each a note—
They can't walk, but they can vote
On the Bochan Bridge of Canso.

Matt MacLean was there, you bet:
He scratched his head and seemed to fret.
His opening speech isn't ready yet
On the Bochan Bridge of Canso.

They were walking two by two
Little Dan and Carroll, too.
And last of all came Donald Boo
O'er the Bochan Bridge of Canso

For people living in the Strait area prior to 1955, transportation by ferry was a way of life. However, dangerous winter crossings, increased traffic, and the general inconvenience of the ferry became the rallying cries residents used to pressure the governments of the day to make a permanent link across the Strait. Back in the fifties, one young man, Thomas Flint, a resident of Saskatchewan, travelled east to find work with CN. In the following letter, Thomas tells of his experiences while working on the train ferry that crossed the Strait of Canso between Mulgrave on the mainland and Point Tupper on the island.

The train ferry Scotia, which crossed between Mulgrave on the mainland to Point Tupper on Cape Breton Island.

## "THE FERRY~A WAY OF LIFE"

I started my career as a CN telegraph operator in Regina in the 1930s. Work was scarce in those days and not having much seniority, I could not hold steady work. In December 1939, I received a call asking if I would go to Nova Scotia. I gladly accepted the invitation and landed in New Glasgow, which would become my headquarters. From there, I worked at many different locations as a spare operator. Two places where I spent a lot of time were Mulgrave and Point Tupper on each side of the Strait of Canso, so I saw a lot of the Strait, crossing it many times on the ferry.

There was no causeway in those days and the coaches and freight cars were taken from one side of the Strait to the other on a ferry. The steam engines (locomotives) were too heavy so they were not taken on the ferry. Instead, they were stationed in Point Tupper for the Sydney run and in Mulgrave for the Truro run.

The ferry had a dining room down below where you could purchase a great all-you-could-eat meal for fifty cents. The crossing would take about thirty to forty minutes depending on the tide in the Strait, giving enough time for a generous meal. Sometimes ice floes, huge in size, would push the ferry a considerable distance down the Strait. Often these huge chunks of ice would pile up on land at the edge of the Strait—quite a sight to see.

I remember one trip when the ferry had the passenger train on it and we were crossing from Mulgrave to Point Tupper. Heavy ice floes pushed the ferry a long dis-

tance down the Strait. It took four hours for it to fight its way back to the landing dock in Point Tupper. I was on it that day and was about three hours late for work.
—Thomas M. Flint

Many others have vivid memories of the ferry. Bernie MacDonald, who grew up in Mulgrave and attended industrial arts classes in Port Hawkesbury, recalls an unusual ferry crossing.

## "ATTEMPTED SUICIDE?"

During my Mulgrave high school days in the early fifties the ninth grade was required to take the "Manual Training" course in Port Hawkesbury. This training, now called "Industrial Arts," was not available in Mulgrave so once a week we would take the car ferry across to Port Hawkesbury for morning shop sessions and then return home for regular school in the afternoon. In Port Hawkesbury, we had become so attuned to the car ferry's schedule that once her whistle sounded for departure we would, with haste that only young legs could muster, drop everything in the shop and run like hell for the stairs, down the hill, across back yards, jumping over fences and the car-ramp barrier, and with a burst of speed and sometimes a short jump from the end of the ramp,

land on the very end of the departing ferry deck.

I remember one day it didn't go exactly that way; having heard the ferry whistle, my friend immediately ran for the shop stairs while I delayed long enough to cover a can of paint. I was soon up to speed, however, and just fifty yards behind him running downhill and jumping fences like an Olympic hopeful. My friend jumped the five-foot gap between the car-ramp and the departing ferry, but by the time I got there the gap had become ten feet. I found out the hard way, and have not forgotten, that my long-jump capability that day was short of Olympian quality. I missed the boat completely, ending up in the churning water, barely missing the ferry deck with my chin, and surfaced at the front edge of the floating dock just inches from being trapped beneath it.

*The ferry terminal in Port Hawkesbury.*

As I clung to what I could, the force of the propeller-driven water pushed me under the floating dock. At that point I heard yelling, the ferry captain cut the engines, and two pair of most welcome arms reached down and pulled me up onto the car-ramp. Unfazed by the near disaster, I looked at the ferry now heading for Mulgrave where a man, stripped to the waist, was poised to jump in after me.

I was disappointed that the ferry did not return for me because the next boat would not leave for an hour. I finally arrived home in Mulgrave, and Mom asked me why I was late; I simply told her the truth—that "I missed the boat," with no attempt at humour. I didn't know at the time of the incident that my brother-in-law had been on that ferry, headed for Mulgrave to visit my mother. When I came home after school, my mother asked me if I had seen anything unusual at the ferry dock in Hawkesbury around 11:30; I told her I had seen nothing unusual. She related to me that my brother-in-law said someone had tried to commit suicide, and I repeated my response that I'd seen nothing like that at all, trying all the while to remember if I had seen anyone running in front of a train or perhaps a car.

By the next day the story was that "this guy jumped into the water and tried to drown himself and two guys grabbed him and stopped him." To myself I was wondering how I could have missed such an event—I had not seen anything of this nature around the time I was there. By the third day, when I came home from school my mother repeated the story with added information, again from my brother-in-law, who told her, "I saw this guy trying to take his life, and if those two men from the dock had not stopped him, he would have succeeded. A man was stripped to his waist on the ferry and was ready to dive in after him." Being an "A" student I was slowly getting the picture, remembering seeing the partially clothed would-be rescuer ready to dive off the departing ferry and save...ME! The strange story that had developed was so bizarre that I had not made the connection between it and me. I told my mother the simple version of this story and while I am sure if gave her some churnings of anxiety, she never spoke of the incident again.
—Bernie MacDonald


Both World War One and World War Two interfered for some time with any progress in the construction of a permanent link. However, high traffic in the Strait, the threat of submarines along the coast, and the sinking of the *Caribou* while on a run from North Sydney to Port aux Basques during World War Two prompted community leaders to take another serious look at the idea of a causeway.

On January 21, 1948, the Honourable Angus L. Macdonald, Premier of Nova Scotia and a Cape Bretoner, along with the Honourable Lionel Chevrier, Federal Minister of Transport, announced the appointment of three engineers to investigate and recommend a type of crossing for the Strait of Canso. With the complete support of Premier Macdonald and the dedicated work of the Canso Crossing Association, the announcement was made in June 1951 that a causeway would be constructed with a proposed budget of $22,000,000. The relocation of the existing highway and railway were projected to cost $3,400,000, while the causeway proper was to cost $9,600,000. The lock and canal system that would allow ships passage through the Strait of Canso would be allotted $5,600,000 and other engineering costs would be in the $3,100,000 range. The government's decision was made after studying the high cost of operating the ferries; its conclusion was that in order for the ferry system to meet traffic needs, maintaining it would cost more than building a causeway.

By now the phrase "to build or not to build" had been bantered about for over one hundred years as people in their communities and various levels of government discussed the idea of building a link to join Cape Breton Island with the mainland of Nova Scotia. And so it was no surprise that the latest plans to build a causeway were met with skepticism. "We'll believe it when we see it!" and "Why bother?" became common refrains. Some thought the idea had as much chance of success as the bridge-building plans of fifty years previous.

The urgent need for a new ferry that could meet the demands of the increase in traffic—coupled with the fact that the passenger ferry, *John Cabot* had a serious accident during one of its crossings—added strength to the people's petitions for a new link.

*The old ferry dock in Port Hawkesbury, at the foot of McSween Street.*

*Mulgrave, circa 1930.*

# CHAPTER 2

# CAUSEWAY CONSTRUCTION

On May 15, 1952, the initial contract for construction of the Causeway was awarded to Northern Construction & J. W. Stewart Limited from Vancouver. Using the rock and fill from adjacent Cape Porcupine to create a causeway, Cape Breton was permanently connected to the mainland on Friday evening, December 10, 1954. The project started in the rain and finished in the rain. According to the souvenir programme, the last load of fill was put in place on December 31, 1954, although the chief engineer of the project, Harry MacKenzie, maintained in later interviews that the last load was put in place on Wednesday December 22, 1954.

The construction of the Canso Causeway was a project on which the federal and provincial governments as well as the railway worked together—a rare occurrence. The work was divided into three phases. The highway was the province's responsibility; the railway was the Canadian National Railway's domain, and the third phase, the building of the canal and waterway, fell under the purview of the federal government.

During ceremonies held on September 16, 1952, to celebrate the first day of construction, sixteen-year-old Eldon Bezanger of Isaacs Harbour was on a steamship, the *Collier*, with his father and his uncle Henry. They were docked at Kingston, Ontario, and happened to be listening to the national news on local radio when across the airwaves came the sound of the first explosion of dynamite at Cape Porcupine. Construction had officially begun.

The transmission of the blast was made possible by a CBC radio broadcast from the work site, thanks partly to the efforts of Earl Peeples from Mulgrave. "Alex Sutherland and I worked for Maritime Tel & Tel. Co. in 1952," says Peeples, "and we ran cable from the bottom of the Cape at the water's edge to the Northern Construction building at the main road for the CBC Radio broadcast so the listening audience could hear when Transportation Minister Hon. Lionel Chevrier pulled the switch to set of the first official blast." Peeples recalls that the opening ceremonies were broadcast from the mainland side in 1952, while the official opening was broadcast from the Cape Breton side three years later.

Many of the men who worked on the construction project were veterans of World War Two. When they came home from the war, they found employment was scarce; there was little demand for their newly acquired skills.

With the announcement of the construction project in the Strait of Canso, men from all over the province, like Bob MacAleese of Parrsboro, were determined to apply for a job. Bob's nephew, Roger Cyr, recalls the memorable trip they made on the back of a motorbike so that Bob could apply for work.

*Roger Cyr with the motorcycle that carried him and his Uncle Bob to Mulgrave in search of employment.*

## "EASY RIDER"

In May of 1952, I purchased a motorcycle and while visiting my aunt and uncle in Parrsboro, my uncle, Bob MacAleese, asked me to give him a ride to Mulgrave, where he wanted to apply for a job building the Canso Causeway. Early on a Friday morning my uncle and I set out with a thermos of coffee and enough baloney sandwiches to last us all day. I was a novice at motorcycle riding and had only once before carried a passenger. I soon learned that it was considerably more difficult negotiating turns in the road as I barely missed hitting a guardrail shortly after starting out. We carried on without further incident and reached Mulgrave just after one o'clock in the afternoon. We sat on the steps of a small building and waited our turn to enter. It began to rain and a cold wind swept down from the Cape Breton highlands, further dampening our spirits. The line was long and slow-moving; when my uncle's turn to enter came, he took me with him for he could see that I was cold and wet. I sat in the background and listened to the interview.

The interviewer was dressed in a three-piece suit. He told us that he was from Guelph, Ontario. "What position would you like to apply for?"

"What do you need?" my uncle replied.

"We need machine operators and diesel mechanics," he was told.

"I have worked with heavy equipment for twenty-five years," my uncle replied, "and have papers for all facets of heavy equipment operations and repair."

I had the impression that the man from Ontario in the three-piece suit was not expecting to find men with such vast experience in Nova Scotia. "Looks like you're the man we have been looking for," he said. "Leave me your name and phone number and someone will be in touch."

We bought coffee at the local restaurant, ate another of our baloney sandwiches and started for Parrsboro. The rain let up a little and we soon reached Antigonish, where the street was under construction. I hit a raised manhole cover with the bike and we were airborne... but I regained control. My motorcycle had a measuring cup attached to the bottom of the gas filler cap where oil was mixed with each tank-full of gasoline. At times since buying the motorcycle I had filled the tank when it was still half full but had always used a full measure of oil, a mistake that would cause us grief as the trip continued towards home.

As we approached Mount Thom on the way into Truro I noticed that we were losing power on the hills. We gassed up at a Texaco station on the corner of Prince and Willow streets, again adding a full measure of oil to a half a tank of gas. By the time we reached Great Village the motorcycle was barely able to maintain thirty miles per hour under full throttle. It continued to misfire and a trail of blue smoke spewed out behind us as we sputtered along.

The bike refused to climb Economy Mountain, even when my uncle got off and we tried it with just me on the bike. By then we had lightened our load of baloney sandwiches, but we were stranded east of the big hill. We phoned Clarence Marsh in Five Islands, loaded the motorcycle on the back of his truck and for two dollars he drove us to Parrsboro.

Too late we discovered that too much oil mixed with the gasoline caused the spark plugs to misfire, resulting in a loss of power. As we sat around the kitchen table discussing our adventure with my aunt, the phone rang. It was the man

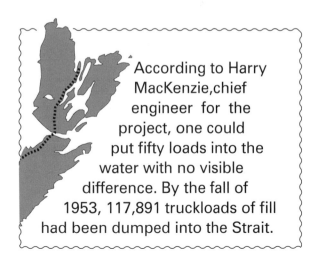

According to Harry MacKenzie, chief engineer for the project, one could put fifty loads into the water with no visible difference. By the fall of 1953, 117,891 truckloads of fill had been dumped into the Strait.

*The road from Aulds Cove to the construction site, with Porcupine Mountain in the background.*

with the three-piece suit calling to tell my uncle that he had a job as a 'dozer' operator. My Uncle Bob worked on the Causeway until the job was completed. He often said the hardest part was getting home from the job interview!
—Roger Cyr

An estimated 9.1 million tonnes of rock was used from neighbouring quarries at Cape Porcupine and approximately 113,400 tonnes of rock was freed with each blast of dynamite. In order to blast these large volumes of granite safely, the engineers would build a T-shaped tunnel system at the face of Cape Porcupine. Once the tunnel was finished, the explosives were set with charge wire, and the tunnel was sealed. Each dynamite blast caused huge amounts of rock to cascade down the moun-

tainside. Once on the ground, these rocks were loaded onto one of the fourteen huge Euclid trucks, then transported to the water's edge where bulldozers nudged the fill to the floor of the Strait of Canso. Progress was slow, especially at first as the tides kept washing the fill away. It took six months to complete the first hundred metres of the Causeway.

Although Cape Porcupine proved to be an excellent source of the rocks and fill needed to construct the Causeway, there was much discussion during the fifties over the price the government paid the Fraser family for this piece of real estate. J. Gordon Ross, Barrister and Solicitor from Kitchener, Ontario, and nephew of the original owner, tells of the legal battle that ensued to settle this debate.

Much of the legal story was provided to Ross by his father's cousin and Uncle Al's son, Duncan Fraser, who currently practises law in Brockville, Ontario. For those who have a particular interest in expropriation law or wish to read in detail the decision of the Exchequer Court and the subsequent appeal to the Supreme Court of Canada, see The Queen ex rel. Deputy Attorney-General of Canada v. Fraser (1960), 23 D.L.R. (2d) 94, and Fraser v. The Queen, [1963] S.C.R. 455.

## "THEY STOLE UNCLE AL'S MOUNTAIN"

In the 1950s and early 1960s, my summer vacations usually included a motor trip. A family station wagon was loaded beyond capacity with kids and luggage for the two- or three-week trip. Having relatives in Northern Ontario, the Prairies and the Maritimes, we alternated between the west and east coasts as destinations.

We were at my dad's sister's summer home near Pictou when the discussion came up about the new Causeway that had recently been completed. As a trip had been planned for the next day to visit my father's aunt, uncle and cousins in Guysborough, it was decided we would take a bit of a detour and look at the new Causeway. Of additional interest was the fact that most of the rock used for the construction of the Causeway came from Porcupine Mountain, located on the south side of the Strait of Canso, about two miles west of Port Hawkesbury. Most of Porcupine Mountain was owned by my father's uncle, Alistair Fraser. Prior to construction, approximately one-third of Porcupine Mountain had been expropriated, and this became a hotly debated issue among members of the family. As kids, we didn't really understand what was going on. We didn't know what the word "expropriated" meant, and we didn't understand the concept of "fair compensation," but we knew something was amiss when we heard comments such as "highway robbery" and "for what they are offering, it's outright theft."

An electric shovel loading rock and fill into a thirty-four-ton Euclid truck at the base of Cape Porcupine.

We crossed the Causeway and from the north side my father and one of my uncles explained the construction of the Causeway and pointed out the quarry operation at Porcupine Mountain. We, of course, had many questions about the "theft." The questions included "Did Uncle Al know they were taking his rocks? Did they take the rocks at night so no one would see them? Did Uncle Al give them permission to come onto his property? Did they pay Uncle Al for the rocks? Did Uncle Al try to stop them?" Interestingly enough, the answer to many of the children's enquiries was "no." That day it became very apparent to my siblings and cousins that someone or some group had indeed stolen Uncle Al's mountain. For fifty years it has been a family story among members of my generation. On each trip to Nova Scotia, we always insisted on a side trip to the Causeway. We wanted to see if any more of Porcupine Mountain had disappeared.

Who was Uncle Al? Alistair Fraser was my great-uncle, and Porcupine Mountain had been acquired by his father, Duncan Fraser, in the late 1880s. Uncle Al was a lawyer who joined the legal department of Canadian National Railway after World War One and later became its general solicitor and counsel. From 1932 until his retirement in 1951, he was a vice-president of the railway. From 1952 to 1958, following in his father's footsteps, he served as lieutenant-governor of Nova Scotia. (Duncan Fraser was lieutenant-governor from 1906 to 1910.) As far as the expropriation proceedings were concerned, he was a rather unique landowner/defendant because of his legal training and his thirty-three years of service with CNR. Being a vice-president in charge of traffic, he was vitally aware of the inadequacies of the ferry service operated by the CNR and of the many studies to correct that problem, studies which had variously recommended an improved ferry service, a tunnel, a low or high level bridge or a causeway.

In December 1950, the Province of Nova Scotia expropriated 110 acres of the 293 acres owned by Uncle Al for the stated purpose of construction, maintenance and repair of a highway. There was no specific mention of construction of the Causeway. In 1951, the federal government continued its studies and decided in June of that year to proceed with the Causeway project, referring specifically to Porcupine Mountain as a source of supply rock in their proposed tender documentation. Later that year, the federal cabinet approved the construction of the Causeway by the Government of Canada.

In June 1952, a construction contract was signed and, interestingly, on July 9, 1952, the Province of Nova Scotia abandoned its expropriation. Fifteen minutes later the federal government expropriated the 110 acres by filing the necessary papers in the land registry office. The Crown confirmed its willingness to pay $5,505.00 for the expropriated property based on a bare market value of $50.00 per acre as waste land. Uncle Al rejected the offer and the matter went before the Exchequer Court of Canada to determine appropriate compensation for the expropriated land. That court ultimately determined that the appropriate compensation would be approximately $40,000. The court determined that a person in the stone quarry business might pay $2,000 to $3,000 per acre to acquire property that would have a potential use as a future quarry. This amount was then applied to the 12.8 acres that had actually been used as the quarry site at Porcupine Mountain.

Uncle Al disagreed with the judgement of the court and the matter was appealed to the Supreme Court of Canada and was ultimately heard in 1963. J. J. Robinette, QC, a well-known and respected barrister from Toronto, was retained for the appeal. The Supreme Court described the reality of the situation as follows: "What was compulsorily taken from the Appellant was intended to be used as a source of building material for which there was an ascertainable market price."

The Court determined that the Appellant was entitled to be paid the fair market value for the quantity of rock taken from the expropriated land. Much evidence was brought forth as to the value of the rock taken, and such values ranged from 4¢ to 10¢ a ton. It was determined that nine million tons had been quarried from the site. A judgement was rendered in favour of Uncle Al in the amount of $360,000 together with interest at 5 per cent from 1952 to 1963, a far cry from the original $5,505 offered eleven years earlier.

I am told that after payment of all legal fees and expenses, Uncle Al gave a significant amount of the judgement to Dalhousie University.

One of the interesting aspects of these proceedings is the possibility this was the first occasion in which an action had been maintained against the Queen by a person who also represented the Queen. Apparently this issue was addressed in a preliminary manner and the Court determined that there was no reason why the proceedings should not continue.

When one looks at the great disparity between the original offer and the ultimate court award, perhaps those original enquiries by the children about the theft and stealing of the rocks had some basis in fact.

A few years ago, on our last trip to Nova Scotia prior to my father's death, we had decided to drive to Louisbourg with a stop in Sydney so that he could show us where he was stationed in the Navy during World War Two. After crossing the Causeway, we stopped at the interpretation centre and while I was attending to a few things, my father started to explain to my children the history of the Causeway and how it was built. A few minutes later as I was walking towards them, I saw my father pointing off in the direction of Porcupine Mountain. As I got closer, I realized the family story was safe for another generation when I heard my youngest daughter ask "But Grandpa, why did they steal Uncle Al's Mountain?"
—J. Gordon Ross

Considering the magnitude of the project, the sheer size of the blasts and the powerful tide action in the Strait of Canso, it is a wonder there weren't many serious accidents during the project. In "A Scary Causeway Story," Bernie MacDonald, who worked on the site as a teenager, remembers one truck's near miss; another Euclid truck driver, Burchell Fulmore, a nineteen-year-old university student, admitted to having a couple of scary experiences while driving his truck over the twisty roads that wind their way down the steep cliffs of Porcupine Mountain.

## "A SCARY CAUSEWAY STORY"

I remember many times standing on the end of the Causeway just to witness the incredible flow of raging water passing by. In its own way, it was just trying to make up for the water level differences

*Men on the Cape Breton side watch the incredible flow of the tide before the gap is closed.*

between one side of the province and the other. As the Causeway advanced and choked off the waterway the flow became more and more angry and began to fight back, not unlike a human fighting for its life.

Originally three quarters of a mile wide, the Strait was becoming more and more restricted as the Causeway pushed itself towards Cape Breton Island. With the tidal flow of water moving through a much narrower slot, the speed at which it traveled increased dramatically, so much so that it eroded the Strait bottom from a depth of 187 feet to 218 feet. There were estimates that at peak water flow, large stones dumped off the end of the Causeway would reach bottom several hundred yards downstream.

This staggering flow and force of water had other effects, including, on occasion, washing away sections of up to 100 feet off the end of the Causeway. It was on one of these occasions that a young mechanic got the scare of this life. His job was to grease the Euclid trucks at the maintenance shop. From time to time at the end of a shift, a truck driver would leave a loaded truck at the maintenance shop, and since trucks had to be empty for greasing, the greaser would drive the truck to the end of the Causeway and dump the load into the water. My friend was doing just that one night when in the process of backing up he felt

the truck tilting backwards. Realizing that a section of the causeway was giving way he shoved the transmission lever into forward and held the accelerator to the floor. After a few seconds of moving neither backward nor forward—seconds that felt like a lifetime—the truck began to move slowly forward up the incline. Once safely on flat ground he shut off the truck engine, climbed down from the cab, and walked home to Mulgrave, never to return to the Causeway again.
—Bernie MacDonald

The dangers of blasting a mountain and building a causeway in deep, fast-flowing water were grave. While the men had their scares and near misses at work, the women and children waited for them at home. Donna Paris tells what it was like to wait for her father's safe return.

## "THE DAY MY FATHER WAS LATE FOR SUPPER"

My father, Cecil Borden from Guysborough, hauled the first load of rock that got the Causeway under construction in 1952, and down through the years how he would glow whenever the subject came up in a conversation. He was forty-one years of age at the time. The cape in 1955 was called Cape Porcupine and that is where they hauled the rocks from. One day while hauling rocks off the cape, my father's truck slid and started tumbling down, coming to rest on a tier below.

My father's brother, Alex Borden, also of Guysborough, ran down to the truck with the other workers. To their amazement, Cecil had survived the fall and jokingly said, "Every time the truck rolled I hung on and when it came to rest on all fours, I was sitting upright."

That was the night he had not come home for supper. In those days supper was at 5:00 P.M., right on the dot. No one ate until everyone was at the table. I remember staying upstairs where I could look out the window and see the end of the driveway and it was well into the evening before he arrived. Of course his main concern was the damaged truck.
—Donna Paris

Cecil Borden

Roger Cyr, who as a boy lived with his grandmother and uncle in Cumberland County, also remembers a story of near disaster on the Causeway. Although he often visited his Uncle Bob at his Causeway job, he did not learn of the accident with the bulldozer until well after the event.

## "BULLDOZER OVER THE CLIFF"

The incident happened on the "A" shift: 12:01 A.M. to 8:00 A.M. Near the end of the ramp where the rocks and fill were dumped sat a "shack" containing the generator that powered the lights which illuminated the construction work area. Bob MacAleese, my uncle, was parked there waiting for trucks to deliver loads of fill for him to push over the end. The machine was running when suddenly the ground gave way and began sliding into the water. He told me he stayed on the machine. He did so

Bob MacAleese

for two reasons: one, he thought it might come to a stop before hitting the water, and the other, if he tried to jump off he might get hit by the machine or the rocks that were tumbling down the slope. He, the shack and the machine slid straight into the water and all were pitched into darkness.

He had a serious situation on his plate: He could be electrocuted from the generator that continued to run, causing sparks to fly in the night air, or he could be swept away with the current. In the end, he escaped unharmed by simply standing on the seat of the dozer, diving clear of it, and swimming ashore.

A few days before this incident, a supervisor had approached him while he was sitting on the machine. In order to hear what the supervisor had to say, Bob attempted to get off and when he did, he snagged the leg of his coverall on one of the steering brake pedals. As he was getting ready to go on shift on the night of the accident, he remembered this and pulled his socks up over his pant legs before putting on his boots. The tight boots around the bottom of his pant leg formed a seal that allowed an air pocket to form, assisting him in floating to the surface when he landed in the water. He told me that if he'd caught his pant leg the night he hit the water he might not have escaped the machine quite so easily.
—Roger Cyr

Colin Purcell, local historian from Mulgrave, added to this story with his comment, "The bulldozer went down fast but the next day Gordie (Yets) MacDonald dove down, put ropes on it and got it out of there. They cleaned it up, dried it off and put it back to work again."

"Dynamiting Old Porcupine" reveals an unexpected side effect the mine blasts had on the fish in the area, an observation Bernie MacDonald made during the summer of 1954, as a seventeen year old who had just completed his first year as a StFX student. He was employed as a miner's helper with Northern Construction and J. W. Stewart Ltd., the main builders of the Canso Causeway.

During the pre-opening days of the Canso Causeway, before activities began for the big day, there was a small stone-crushing and -trucking operation in progress in the area. This involved a gravel-crushing operation near Havre Boucher and the trucking of the crushed stone to a stockpile in Aulds Cove, close to where the Causeway roadbed turns left across the Strait. Bernie MacDonald's job was to weigh the trucks at the platform scalehouse before they dumped their load and returned to the crusher in Havre Boucher.

## "DYNAMITING OLD PORCUPINE"

The miner's job was to tunnel deep into Porcupine Mountain and, using dynamite, bring down large sections of broken rock to be used as fill for the Causeway base. The stone fill was trucked and dumped into the Strait in large Euclid diesel trucks hired for that purpose only.

The continuous hard-rock mining operation started with tunnelling: We drilled and blasted cave-like tunnels straight into the mountain using air-compressor-driven, diamond-bit drilling equipment. The tunnels were about six feet in height and five feet in width—big enough for two men to work drill-

*Blasting Cape Porcupine*

ing equipment at the rock face. While air power was used to drive the rotating drills into the rock face, water was run through the centre of the drill shaft and bit to reduce and wash away the stone dust that was generated by the rotating and grinding of the powerful diamond bits. As miners, our clothing consisted primarily of steel-toed rubber boots, waterproof overalls and jacket, plus a mandatory hard hat with a miner's light. The light was connected to a large battery pack via a cord that was clipped around the hard hat and down over the back of the waterproof jacket. The battery pack was held in place by a large leather belt strapped around the waist and buckled in the front. Waterproof gear was necessary because of the water used in the drilling equipment. Plus, an almost constant trickle of water weeped from the tunnel roof.

The large drilling equipment weighed over one hundred pounds and because we were drilling into a vertical rock face, an adjustable pneumatic support leg was needed to hold up the jackhammer. This leg not only supported the weight of the hammer, it also provided thrust to drive the rotating bit deep into the rock face. Because of the size and weight of the equipment the long drill bit had to be physically held in place to start the hole; if the bit wasn't held in place it would simply slide and dance over the surface of the rock face, not unlike trying to

start a running electric drill into a piece of metal. Until the drill bit was "started" or "collared," it was physically held in place at the rock face with the bare hands of the miner's helper, an action that was repeated over and over during an eight-hour shift. Protective gloves could not be worn because of the risk of the gloves being caught around the rotating drill shaft. A caught glove could mean broken wrists or arms, or worse. Needless to say, this bare-hand work was dangerous, messy, and over time built up very tough and thick calluses, so much so that I could actually put a cigarette butt out on my calluses.

The tunnels were drilled and blasted directly into the mountain face; small blasts of fifty pounds were set off several times a week as we dug deeper into the mountain to a pre-determined depth. Several shorter tunnels were drilled and blasted at right angles to the main tunnels so that the final tunnel configuration looked like a "T," "E" or "F," or a combination of all three. The main dynamite loads that were blasted every month or so were not loaded into the main tunnels, which would mostly drive all the backfill out of the main tunnel and not bring down very much rock, but into these side tunnels.

On blasting days everything came out of the quarry. All personnel and equipment were moved about a half-mile away to the main office and maintenance area for the blast. I personally went into the maintenance garage and hid under the large thick steel box of a Euclid truck.

Because of the magnitude of the blast there were a number of small rocks that made it to the office area, but there was never, to my knowledge, any damage to buildings or equipment. What was interesting, however, was the momentary impact the shock wave of the blast had on the fish along the shoreline. The water's edge was less than a few hundred yards from the blast face and the shock wave that went through the water momentarily stunned hundreds of fish which, unconscious and having lost control of their swim bladder, floated to the surface of the water. Codfish, haddock, and pollack were there for the taking; a few people remembered to bring long-handle dip nets for this purpose. Within moments the stunned fish would recover and swim away—until the next big blast. Regardless, it was the best fishing I have ever done, and for the record, it was the first and last time I ever went fishing with explosives! —Bernie MacDonald

"The role of women on the [construction] project was that of support to their husbands," says Isabel Harling, wife of Ellsworth Harling, who was a surveyor with the consulting engineering firm and was involved with the project from beginning to end. Edna Phelan agrees with this statement. Her husband was part of the paving team that worked during the last six months of the project. She couldn't remember any women working on the site except those in the office. Of her own life at that time, she spoke of the fourteen other families who lived in a community of trailers in Aulds Cove. "We didn't have running water, but the friendships we formed have lasted a lifetime."

Some of the women who watched their husbands leave for their shifts on construction lived in fear of never seeing their husbands again. Theresa Hill from Arichat remembers a time when she was wakened from a deep sleep, sure she heard her husband's truck in the driveway then his key in the door. Little did she know he was at that same moment buried by a rock fall during a blast. Theresa's daughter, Gloria Hill, recounts the story in "Something Went Wrong."

## "SOMETHING WENT WRONG"

My dad, Angus Hill (1924–1995), was born in Balmoral, Richmond County. He was a carpenter by trade but was multi-talented. He married my mother and moved to Janvrin's Island at the age of twenty-six. His father-in-law (known to us kids as Pop-Pop) was a fisherman and Dad used to fish with him. In the winter, Dad would cut firewood, mend lobster pots and fishing gear and work wherever he could find it.

One of these winter jobs was on the Canso Causeway project to create a road over one of the deepest ice-free waterways, and he was very proud of his contribution. Dad worked as a labourer, and was chosen to be one of the blast men because he had experience with dynamite. He had to set the explosives used to loosen the rock from Porcupine Mountain. It was his turn to work the graveyard shift (midnight to 8:00 A.M.) one

*Blasters on the Cape Breton side of the Causeway.*

night and he was once again on Porcupine Mountain. Something went wrong and the rock face caved in, trapping him behind a wall of rock.

At the same time my mother was in bed on Janvrin's Island. She heard his car come up in the yard, his key in the door, and his footsteps padding down the hall and into their bedroom. When she opened her eyes she expected to see him standing in the doorway, but she was alone—it was just her and their two young sons. On the job site, a bulldozer cleared the entranceway to the cave and my dad exited, unharmed, but shook up.

The next morning they shared their experiences and speculated about the implications of this forerunner. My mother has never had a similar experience since.

Dad always claimed he was one of the first people to cross the Causeway. He was riding on the tandem truck that made the last load to actually connect the two sides and the tandem crossed over the newly created road from one side to the other. After his work with the Canso Causeway, he went to Port aux Basques, Newfoundland, to work on the Marine Atlantic ferry terminal.
—Gloria Hill

Sadly, two lives were lost during the construction: a young man named Philip Joseph Ryan was killed while working on the canal phase of the project. Only pieces of his story have emerged to date but apparently he was driving a truck, filling in for a friend who was being married that day, when he suffered a fatal injury. The other recorded fatality was of George Stewart White, a driller who was killed in one of the blasts on the mountain. His daughter Florence Cook has only a faded black and white photo and a few fond memories of her father. She shares them in "The Death of Me."

George Stewart White, killed during the construction of the Causeway while drilling on Cape Porcupine.

## "THE DEATH OF ME"

"That place is going to be the death of me," my father, George Stewart White, told his neighbour just days before he died while working on the construction of the Canso Causeway. Born in Goldboro on November 30, 1899, my father moved our family to Havre Boucher when he found work as a driller on "the mountain"—which is what the miners called their work site on Porcupine Mountain. Perhaps his premonition was a result of the three separate accidents he'd had while working on the project. He'd lost a thumb, broken several ribs and suffered a head injury when a rock went through his hardhat and split his head open.

After his third accident, he was made a spotter at the end of the Causeway where the Euclid trucks were dumping their loads. However, it was a cold and lonely job standing out on the end of a causeway holding a light and he longed for the familiar: drilling the rock on the mountain. So, as soon as he healed, he went back to the job he knew best.

On the morning of February 28, 1954, I woke to the sound of my mother crying in the kitchen. It must have been a weekend, because I wasn't at school. Grandma met me in the hall and she told me to go back into my room, but I was headstrong and I pushed past her. I had to get to my mother. I remember seeing two men standing in the kitchen. One was a foreman from the work site and the other a minister.

My father's untimely death left my mother and five children to grieve our loss. I was twelve at the time and the youngest child was two and a half. Mother received a small pension after the accident, and with the help of the community, which took up a collection to help the family, she was able to buy a house for three hundred dollars back in Goldboro. Mom was forty-two when my dad died. She never liked us to talk about him because it made her cry. Father is buried in Bay View Cemetery, Goldboro. —Florence Cook

As early as August 1954, the tide rushing through the narrowing gap made navigation hazardous to shipping. At this time, the government considered banning passage for ships over 150 feet in length. Cutting through the Strait of Canso saved 130 miles of travel, and during the last summer before construction was completed, several ships tried to make it

*The project near completion, when fast-moving tides washed away the fill almost as fast as it was unloaded.*

through the gap even though the swift running tides gained in strength as the Causeway moved its toe towards Cape Breton Island. Earlier in the year one skipper had his 10,000-ton freighter damaged by rocks in an attempt to avoid an early morning current on the Cape Breton side. When questioned about the incident, he was reported to say, "The mountain in the sea changed what the charts recorded."

Several people shared memories of an incident that took place on November 29, 1954, around nine-thirty in the evening. The 2,200-ton Norwegian freighter MV *Lionne*, on its way from Virginia to Prince Edward Island for a load of potatoes, ground to an unexpected halt as it fetched up on the Causeway. The incident occurred just ten days before the connecting load of fill linking the mainland to Cape Breton was put in place. Apparently the captain of the freighter was sailing full steam ahead through the Canso Strait and was surprised to see a string of bright lights ahead. Too late to stop, he rammed the Causeway head-on. The noise from the impact startled residents on both sides of the Strait.

When Harry MacKenzie, chief engineer of the project heard the ship was aground, he went up to the Causeway and discovered Captain Josef P. Torreson walking on the fill. During their meeting the captain was reported to have said, "If I go fast, I yump over it!" Bill Covey, then a cartographer for the Canadian Hydrographic Service in Ottawa, where it was his job to help produce Canada's Marine Navigation Charts, wrote, "The ship was using an outdated British Admiralty chart which did not show the new Causeway. If they had updated their Admiralty chart, or purchased the latest Canadian Hydrographic Service chart, the Causeway would have been shown. We got a chuckle out of the incident, particularly when the insurer of the ship tried to sue the Admiralty and the Hydrographic Service for not having the Causeway on their charts." Captain Torreson protested that his chart, bought May 30 in Oslo, indicated it was safe for him to go through the Strait. However, the Canadian Department of Transport's reaction to this suggestion was, "The ship had no business being in the Strait at all." Shipping had been closed since November 17, 1954. Fortunately, none of the twenty-six crew members were injured and when Arthur Langley, Jr. made the underwater survey, he discovered no serious damage to the hull.

The incident happened about ten days prior to the last loads of fill being put in place; one can only imagine the devastation and possible loss of life if the structure had been a bridge rather than a causeway.

From the turn of the last century until 1955, the island's residents depended on a transportation system that combined the ferry and railway systems to deliver goods to and from the island. The railway was particularly important, as it was used to transport coal and steel produced in the Sydney and industrial area of Cape Breton.

Another influence on the decision to build a causeway, complete with a road, a lock, and

The Norwegian Freighter MV Lionne aground on the Causeway.

train tracks, was the fact that Newfoundland and Labrador (then called Newfoundland) officially became part of Canada on March 21, 1949. This made for additional movement of goods and services through Cape Breton.

The construction of the railway was under the supervision of Construction Superintendent R. K. DeLong of Moncton, New Brunswick. The Wasson Construction Company Ltd. of Saint John, New Brunswick, was responsible for the construction of the Cape Breton approaches, and Atlantic Construction Company of Moncton constructed the approaches on the mainland side. The completion of the railway brought an end to the uncertainty, long delays and restricted traffic of the ferry system and meant more regular and quicker deliveries to and from the industries on the island. Another benefit to Canadian National Railways was the elimination of the steep grades on the mainland side of the Strait, thus reducing operating costs and increasing revenue from the greater volume of traffic.

Directly across from Cape Porcupine, Balache Point conveniently protruded into the Strait of Canso; because of its position, this point was chosen as the most suitable place to construct a canal and lock system to allow ships to continue their journey through the Strait. Although this second and third phase of construction was less substantial than the construction of the Causeway, the engineering was more detailed and complex. The T. C. Gorman Construction Company, under the direction of general superintendent Remi Laroque and engineer Lester Williams, was responsible for this phase of the project. The berths for mooring ships, the canal and the locks measure a total of 1202 metres (3,945 feet) while the canal is 570 metres (1,870 feet) long, 24.4 metres (80 feet) wide with a distance of 250 metres (820 feet) between

*The CNR crew laying track, December 14, 1954.*

the gates. These particular gates were selected because of their ability to resist water pressure and ice from both sides.

Space behind the cofferdam and straight-wall pilings was filled with earth and stone excavated from the canal and a total of 76,455 cubic metres (100,000 cubic yards, or roughly 400,000,000 pounds) of concrete was used while the walls, sills, bridges and foundations of the canal were being built

Still in use, the 94-metre (308-foot), 909-tonne swing bridge rotates on a 96.5-centimetre (38-inch) pivot. Machinery to operate the swinging bridge is controlled from a cabin on the second floor of the bridge. The swing takes less than a minute and a half to complete. The bridge, a vital link for transportation, incorporates a highway, a railway, and a canal to enable shipping to operate through the Strait of Canso.

The companies involved in the bridge's construction were representative of the whole country. Two companies from Vancouver were responsible for the construction of the

The National Geographic Traveler Destination Scorecard for the spring of 2004 puts Cape Breton Island in second place in a world survey for sustainable tourism, destination stewardship and related fields.

Causeway and the shore approaches from the mainland side. Maritime Steel and Foundries Limited, New Glasgow, Nova Scotia, built the bridge and gates for the canal, a Quebec company was responsible for building the lock system and the highway approaches from Cape Breton, and consulting engineers on the project worked for O. J. McCulloch Engineering Company of Montreal.

Cape Porcupine, with its vast quantities of granite rock well-suited for fill as it is impregnable to water, provided all the rock for the Causeway project. The rip-rap which protects the fill from being washed away by heavy tides consists of boulders having a minimum weight

*Workmen and equipment laying the train tracks on the Island side of Causeway during the construction phase.*

*Porcupine Mountain during lock construction.*

of four tons. As the time of the 1955 opening neared, leading politicians and businessmen were asked to comment on the great achievement; all agreed it deserved the admiration of every Canadian. C. D. Howe said, "The Canso Causeway has been built by man despite tide and storm and the hazard of a depth of water never before encountered in such an undertaking." Claire Gillis, Cape Breton South Member of Parliament, remarked, "Bringing this project to fruition demonstrates than one can get anything one wants in this world provided he doesn't care who gets the credit for it."

And statesman George Drew predicted that the completion of the Causeway would draw people from all over the world: "The existence of the Canso Causeway will make readily accessible to all Canadians the magnificent highland scenery of the Island. I look forward to the time when the Island will be well-known, not only to Canadians, but to friendly visitors from other countries who will be impressed to observe how carefully the customs and traditions of the Island have been preserved over the years."

Nearly fifty years later, despite the ravages of winds, tides and ice, the Causeway continues to be a significant structure. By 1957, an average of 760 vehicles per day crossed the Causeway and 1,273 ships per year navigated the canal. In 2002, approximately 8040 vehicles per day and 2,042 ships per year used this transportation system designed and completed a half century ago.

*A construction scene during the building of the 4000 foot canal and lock system at the Causeway.*

# CHAPTER 3

# FIRSTS

## (AND LASTS)

Once completed, the Canso Causeway was the deepest man-made structure of its type in the world at a depth of 66 metres (218 feet) and a span of 1310.6 metres (4300 feet). At eighty feet wide, it provides room for a twenty-four-foot highway section, a single-tract railway, and a six-foot sidewalk, with lights and railings separating each. Like an iceberg, it is about eight times wider on the ocean floor than it is at its crest. The decision to make a narrower crest came after the engineers considered the severity of the storms and ice movements in the area. A narrower crest, bolstered by armour rock, would improve resistance against the powerful attacks of ice and wind.

A number of people have claimed their place in Causeway history as one of the "firsts": first to think of a causeway, first to walk, drive, pay a toll, ride, protest, or pipe across the Causeway. While many such claims have been passed down through family stories and local lore, only those that are documented are truly dependable. Most of the firsts included here, therefore, are from archives, museums, newspapers and other periodicals of the day.

+**FIRST FERRY SERVICE:** As early as 1819 Hugh MacMillan used small dories to ferry people from MacMillan Point on the Island across the Strait to Cape Porcupine on the mainland. In the winter Mr. MacMillan ferried mail and passengers across the Strait by horse and sleigh, and in 1929 he petitioned the government to grant him enough money to keep a comfortable ferry for men and cattle. The MacMillans' service was passed on for three generations and was one of the reasons that "MacMillan Causeway" was considered as a possible name for the new Causeway in 1955.

+ **FIRST TRAIN TO CROSS THE STRAIT:** Although its first scheduled trip wasn't until June 2, 1892, the first train to run from New Glasgow to Sydney arrived on November 24, 1890. It crossed the Strait from Mulgrave to Point Tupper on Nova Scotia's pioneer steel ship, a barge-like ferry called SS *Mulgrave*.

+ **FIRST SCOTIA FERRY CROSSING:** The coal-fired ship *Scotia I* made its first crossing of the Strait on April 25, 1902, replacing its predecessor, the SS *Mulgrave*. Later, because of increased traffic during the war, *Scotia I* was joined by a sister ship, the *Scotia II*. Both ships were equipped with ice-breaking equipment and carried nine Pullman cars on the three-tracked deck. The total purchase price paid by the Intercolonial Railway for one ferry was the significant sum of $289,435. The ferries were kept busy with four express trains per day, two in each direction.

The crossing, together with the re-coupling of the engines that were left at the docks on each side of the Strait, usually took about an hour to complete. Although the ferries had a top speed of about nine knots, they were often hampered by the swift running tides of up to six knots and ferry workers remember long

delays getting into port during periods of bad weather.

• **FIRST GOVERNMENT RECOGNITION OF THE APPARENT NEED FOR A CANSO CROSSING:** According to Premier Connolly, the apparent need for a Canso crossing was first presented in the Nova Scotia legislature in 1937 when the attorney general of Nova Scotia, Honourable Malcolm Patterson, introduced a resolution calling on the federal government to take steps to build a crossing at the Strait of Canso, be it a bridge, causeway or a tunnel.

*The completed Causeway as seen from the mainland.*

• **FIRST STRAIT OF CANSO COM-MITTEE:** A committee consisting of M. R. Chappell, W. S. Wilson, Roland MacIntyre and L. J. Doucet of Sydney; Johnston Chew and Dan A. MacDonald of Glace Bay; I. N. MacLean of New Waterford; and Allistair MacDonald of Louisburg formed in April 1947 with the intention of promoting the Canso project. Later in the month this committee had a meeting with Premier Angus L. Macdonald to ask if the province would contribute to the cost of a crossing and represent the committee's requests to the federal government in Ottawa.

• **FIRST DECISION TO BUILD THE CANSO CAUSEWAY:** On June 27, 1951, newspapers reported the Board of Engineers was recommending the construction of a $22,769,000 stone causeway and a navigation lock on the Cape Breton side of the Causeway located behind Balache Point.

• **ROAD TO THE ISLES FIRST COMPLETED:** On the last night of filling, Harry MacKenzie, resident engineer, said they rolled boulders into the Strait that were half the size of a room and the tides were so swift that the fill kept washing away. After a three-year wait, the final truckload of rock linking Canada to Cape Breton was unloaded around 8:30 P.M. on Friday, December 10, 1954.

• **FIRST TO CROSS:** Angus Hill claimed to be one of the first people to cross the Causeway. He was riding on the tandem truck that made the last load to actually connect the two sides and the tandem crossed over the newly created road from one side to the other.

W. L. (Bill) Rudderham wrote the following account of his adventuresome uncle, Bernie Rudderham, an ironworker who lived on the Rudderham Road in Point Edward. Bernie was the first to make the trip west and east on the causeway on the same day:

"Several workmen on the Cape Breton side were watching the filling operation where the large trucks were dumping huge rocks and the dozers were pushing the material into the ever-closing gap. As the gap narrowed, the workmen on the Cape Breton side kept edging closer to watch the rocks as they nestled into place and came closer to the surface. Finally, one Cape Bretoner said, "I think I can make it now!" He jumped down on the rocks and half-wading, half-running made it to the other side—all the while dodging rocks being dumped from the next truck. Others followed. Once safely on the Nova Scotia mainland, this first adventurer had the forethought to scramble back down, still dodging rocks, and head for the Cape Breton side. Thus, he was the first man to make the trip both west and east on the same day. He was also hightailing it away from the company's safety inspector, who wasn't ready to risk the dangerous journey, one we all take for granted today.

• **FIRST TO DRIVE ACROSS:** On December 11, 1955, the morning after the connecting load of fill was put in place, the resident engineer in charge of the project's supervision and design for O. J. McCulloch, Ltd., Harry MacKenzie of Dartmouth, arrived in the office after his trip across on the ferry from Mulgrave. He invited his secretary, Tinker MacDonald, the office manager, Gerry Doane, and the instrument man, Harlene, to go for a ride. When they asked him where they were going, he responded, "We're going over to Canada." After inching his way across the cofferdam, the group crossed the Causeway, and made the trip by road to Mulgrave where they caught the ferry back to the Island to complete the first round trip.

Three days later, on December 13, 1954, three veterans of the Causeway crossing project drove their cars from the Cape Breton side to the mainland. The men were Harry MacKenzie, Vincent Delorey and Les Williams (Delorey and Williams were engineers for T. C. Gorman, Ltd. on the Port Hastings part of the job). However, the Causeway wasn't opened to the public until May of 1955. The Victoria–Inverness Bulletin reported one week earlier that the Strait fiercely resisted being filled in while Lieutenant-Governor Alistair Fraser and approximately fifty people from both sides of the Strait stood in mud and drizzle to watch the last load of fill being put in place.

John Diefenbaker and his entourage met the first work train to cross the new Causeway. L–R: Dr. Gordon MacDonald, Sydney physician; Ned Manson, Sydney businessman and later a cabinet minister in the Stanfield provincial government; Mr. Diefenbaker; D. Stuart Macleod, a Sydney businessman; and Walter Colhoun, a Sydney businessman.

18, 1955, travelling from Cape Breton to the mainland for five cars of road ballast. Apparently, Tory party leader John Diefenbaker was in Sydney at the time and when his workers heard the historic crossing was about to happen, they rushed Diefenbaker and his entourage to the Causeway in time to meet the train and greet the crew. Photos of the train and "the Chief" were taken, but the Grits, who were in power in 1955, were not altogether happy to see Diefenbaker being connected to the event when his picture appeared in the papers the next day.

### • FIRST WORK TRAIN CROSSING:
A work train crossed the Causeway on April

### • THE LAST RUN OF THE TRAIN
FERRY: Frank O'Neil was the skipper on

the last run of the train ferry, *Scotia II* on May 14, 1955. Angus Currie says he was the first train passenger to cross the Canso Causeway, while Martin Boston and his friend Jim Mac-Donnell bought the last two tickets on the last train ferry out of Point Tupper.

Martin Boston, now living in Blues Mills and curator of the Orangedale train station, doesn't remember a time when he wasn't fascinated by a train, so it was natural for him to want to be a passenger on the last train to leave Cape Breton.

## "A TREK BY TRAIN"

On May 14, 1955, my friend Danny MacDonnell and I each bought a ticket for $1.00 and boarded the passenger train in Point Tupper, pulled by Engine #5270 out of Sydney. The full train and engine crossed over to Mulgrave on the ferry *Scotia II*. My plan was to be a passenger on the first passenger train to come across the newly completed Causeway, crossing from mainland Nova Scotia onto Cape Breton Island.

I bought the last ticket sold at the Point Tupper station but at eighteen I was stupid; when the conductor came along and asked for my ticket, I gave it to him and he kept it. I was so dejected. I should have bought another ticket to keep as a souvenir.

After crossing to the mainland we met and boarded the train at Monastery for our historic crossing across the Strait. Engine #6014 East pulled the first passenger train across the Causeway and into the station in Port Hawkesbury, where Danny and I disembarked.

The 6014 was the first Mountain-type engine to arrive on Cape Breton. Prior to the completion of the Causeway, these engines were too heavy to run on the Scotia ferries so they were stationed in Mulgrave. However, shortly after the first one came across, six more were stationed on the island. I don't think the enormity of the situation really sunk in back then. But the opening of the Causeway disrupted a way of life. The railway terminals at Point Tupper and Mulgrave closed, and jobs became scarce. The towns around the Strait took a long time to recover.
—Martin Boston

✦FIRST PASSENGER TRAIN: H. G. Clough was the engineer on the first mainland to Cape Breton run, May 14, 1955.

✦LAST CNR TRAIN: On October 1, 1993, Train #407 was the last CNR train to cross the Causeway from Cape Breton to the mainland. Driver: Conrad Clark; Conductor: E. W. Ross; Brakeman: Kevin Musgrave. The train consisted of five diesel engines, thirty-five cars and one caboose.

+ **FIRST COMMERCIAL VEHICLE TO CROSS:** Although no date was given, John Dunbar claims he was driving a truck for Sydney Transfer in 1955 and drove the first commercial vehicle over the Causeway from Cape Breton to the mainland. An 18 x 11 inch advertisement in the Post Record announced: "Another First!! By Sydney Transfer. Sydney Transfer and Storage Limited Are Proud To Have Made The First Commercial Use of the Canso Causeway."

+ **FIRST COMMERCIAL VEHICLE TO PAY A TOLL:** Although there were twelve cars ahead of him, Gerry Cooke from Truro

*Gerry Cooke and the first commercial vehicle to pay a toll.*

paid the first toll for the first commercial vehicle going through the toll booths from Cape Breton to the mainland. After spending many years as a bus driver for Acadian Coach Lines, the opening of the Causeway meant Mr. Cooke would no longer be subjected to the often treacherous winter rides on the ferry. His wife, Gladys, said he came home and passed her the ticket and told her she might want to keep it.

+ **FIRST CASH CUSTOMERS:** On May 20, 1955, Gib Whitney and his dance band, Frank Dobranski, Tony Lannon, Charley Hillcoat, Jim (Shoo) Shea and John Nearing, were the first cash customers at the gateway to cross the Causeway to Cape Breton. They were returning to the island after playing at the convocation at St. Francis Xavier University. As they neared the toll booths going into Cape Breton, they were held up by the RCMP and an assortment of dignitaries, journalists and media, who told them they were the first paying customers. The toll was seventy-five cents each way. Charles G. Fitzpatrick, a piper from New Glasgow, didn't arrive in time to precede the first car, but he still walked across, proudly playing the pipes.

+ **FIRST BUS TO CROSS:** Joe Boyle, a driver for Acadian Lines, drove the first bus across the Causeway on May 20, 1955. He is pictured in front of his bus in the August 10, 1955, *Post Record* accompanied by "a lassie in highland dress," Miss Donna Hall of Sydney.

**• FIRST HIGH SCHOOL CLASS TO WASH THE CAUSEWAY:** Dwayne MacDonald, a former student of Judique-Creignish High School, wrote, "I was always very good at coming up with ways and ideas for missing a bit of class time, and my parents had just had a conversation with me about how much I could achieve if I would just apply myself, so I applied myself and set out to come up with the ultimate idea for bringing the grand prize (a giant pink sneaker) to Judique-Creignish High School." On May 29, 1985, MacDonald and a group of students from the school washed the Causeway (and everything else in their way) with brushes. The activity was in response to a challenge to see which school would earn the title of the Most Outlandish Group Activity (MOGA Madness) in order to win the Pink Sneaker Award.

*Donna Louise, the first commercial boat to go through the canal.*

*Moga Madness on the Causeway. L–R: Gary MacDougall, Laura Ashford, unknown, Johanna MacIsaac (with sign), Kim MacDonald (Hartery), Ian MacEachern (behind Kim), Bill MacDougall.*

Official Opening Day    August 13/55

*About 40,000 people gathered to celebrate the opening of the Causeway, August 13, 1955.*

# CHAPTER 4

# THE OPENING OF THE CANSO CAUSEWAY:

## AUGUST 13, 1955

On opening day, islanders from all cultural backgrounds joined in extending a welcome to all those around them. One man said, "It was like a handshake across the water, a handshake whose clasp remained! It was a scene to inspire understanding and goodwill."

During the ceremonies, the famous march of the pipers, The MacDonald Hundred, the tartans, the highland dancers, the images decorating the souvenir programme and the lyrics printed on the back of the programme bore testimony to the island's Scottish heritage. The programme included a tree-of-life border design, derived from the Greek acanthus leaf found in the Nova Scotia coat of arms, as well as a stylized animal head, an ornament based on the forms of animals, birds and reptiles. The thistle—emblematic of Scotland—was also used, the lettering was in an ancient Celtic style. The programme was printed in red, yellow, light blue, dark blue, black and gold, and included the words to the

*"THE ROAD TO THE ISLES":*

*Sure, by Tummel and Lock Rannoch and Lochaber I will go,*
*By heather tracks wi' heaven in their wiles;*
*If it's thinkin' in your inner heart braggart's in my step,*
*You've never smelt the tangle o'the Isles.*
*Oh the far Coolins are puttin' love on me,*
*As step I wi' my cromak to the Isles.*

song, "The Road to the Isles": The impressive celebrations on August 13, 1955, were started with one hundred pipers marching across the Causeway playing "The Road to the Isles"—as had been the dream of the late premier of the province, Hon. Angus L. Macdonald. Although Macdonald had not lived to see his dream fulfilled, having passed away on April 21, 1954, his spirit was felt in the hearts of all

Highland dancers, members of the RCMP, and pipers received certificates as a thank-you for participating in the opening. Sueanne Meagher and her sister, Cora, were among the highland dancers that followed the pipe band across the causeway

HMCS Quebec, one of only two Royal Canadian Navy cruisers at the time, sailing up the Strait on the day of the opening.

that attended the ceremonies. Many admitted to having a lump in their throat or a tear trickle down their cheek as the skirl of the pipes echoed and resounded across the Strait of Canso. Two other men who contributed to the construction of the Causeway were also missing at the opening ceremonies: Dr. D. S. Ellis and Thomas Moore. Ellis, former Dean of Engineering at Queen's University, Kingston, Ontario, completed the initial survey of the Strait of Canso and recommended the building of the Causeway. He died a few months before the completion of the project. Moore, the Office Engineer for the Department of Transport, died in January 1955.

The major event of the afternoon occurred at 2:25 as Trade Minister C. D. Howe finished his inaugural address and slashed a tartan ribbon with a claymore used at the Battle of Culloden. After the salute by the Air Force and the Royal Canadian Navy to the late premier, the pipers, led by Sylvia Shore from Glace Bay, began the famous march across the Causeway. Angus L.'s place at the head of the procession was left vacant but his widow, Catherine (MacDougall) Macdonald, Lieutenant.-Governor Alistair Fraser and his wife, Jane (Ross), CNR president Donald Gordon and Trade Minister C. D. Howe, carrying crook-shaped cromachs, led the dignitaries. Newspapers all across Canada showed images of twenty-five lines of pipers and the estimated 40,000 people who took part in the celebration.

"Dhutaich Fhein—My Own Land" pays tribute to former premier Angus L. Macdonald, who died one year before the opening of the Causeway linking his beloved island to the mainland.

## DHUTAICH FHEIN—MY OWN LAND
### HILTON MCCULLY

See that lone, fog-shrouded shieling
On the bonny Breton shore;
Think of how you might have reached it
In the trying days of yore.
The Canso tides were racy,
The ice was bitter hell,
But this has all been altered
By the dream of Angus L.

He dreamed a hundred pipers
Were marching four abreast,
All up and down a causeway
Which linked the East and West.

Their kilts were Scotia's tartan,
And the skirling pipes and shrill
Told both of roaring battles
And the ripple of the rill.

With sweetest of all music,
His dream was not in vain,
The "Flowers O' the Forest"

And the loved "Mo Dhutaich Fhein."
He heard these notes, this dreamer,
And his dream we must applaud,
Tho' no longer in his ain land is his home,
But with his God.

In tribute to his memory,
His dream is now complete,
And when the seer and poet
To write with words replete,

The story of the causeway
And how it all befell,
Takes up his pen and paper,
Let silence for a spell,

For just a quiet moment,
Break in the noisy vein
In tribute to his courage...
He loved "Mo Dhutaich Fhein."

The pipers who played at the opening remember well the famous march across the Canso Causeway. However, the organizing committee invited only one hundred pipers to be the official participants, and this left a number of pipers—some of whom had gone to unusual lengths to make sure they were part of the celebrations—a bit disgruntled. One man purchased a set of pipes from Scotland especially for the occasion, but when he realized his name hadn't been selected, he drove from Halifax early in the morning before the ceremonies began and marched to the island to the sound of his new pipes.

A. W. R. MacKenzie from the Gaelic College and John Kennedy from Inverness were also disappointed by the organizing committee's decisions. For two years Mackenzie had been promoting the idea that the Gaelic College's "Macdonald Hundred" Junior Pipe Band, made up of young people studying at the college, should lead the parade at the official opening of the Canso Causeway. He had renamed the band in honour of the late premier and his dream of having one hundred pipers perform at the official opening. The organizing committee, however, had determined that the parade should be led by male pipers, with the Gaelic College pipe band and other junior bands taking a less prominent role. After protests, the committee finally gave permission for the Junior Girls' Pipe Band to participate as a unit in the line of march as part of the second "one hundred" pipers.

Although the number of pipers at the opening has sometimes been disputed, confirmation that there were more than one hundred pipers may be found in the special instructions given to each participant on the day of the opening: "The first hundred pipers will move forward leaving space for the official guests to line up for the historic march. The second hundred pipers will then follow. Note: The march extends for a good 'Scottish' mile. C. D. Howe will give the inaugural address and will cut a NS tartan ribbon." All of the junior bands were relegated to what was called the "second one hundred" and marched across behind the combined men's bands. Karen Wood of Glace Bay and her cousin Sheila carried the Gaelic College MacDonald One Hundred Pipe Band banner and led their

*The Sydney Girl's Pipe Band on the day of the opening.*

band in the parade across the Canso Causeway at its official opening.

The junior bands marched one behind the other and took turns playing. As one band played once through "The Road to the Isles" and then "The Hundred Pipers," they stopped playing and the band behind them struck up and played the same tunes. Each of the eight junior bands would play before the cycle would be repeated from the front. The order of parade of the junior bands in the second one hundred was determined by each band's formation date, as follows: The New Glasgow Ceilidh Club Girls' Pipe Band, The Gaelic College "Macdonald Hundred" Senior, Junior, and Juvenile Pipe Bands, The Dunvegan Girls' Pipe Band of Westville, The Stellarton Balmoral Girls' Pipe Band, The MacDougall Girls' Pipe Band (Glace Bay), The Truro Girls' Pipe Band, The Stornaway Junior Pipe Band, The Sydney Academy School Pipe Band, and Sydney Girls Pipe Band.

In the end, MacKenzie was to take some satisfaction in his band's performance: the seventy-two Gaelic College band members came through the hot, three-mile march with flying colours. A top ranking CNR official honoured their pipe band by awarding them "Top Performance" among the twenty-five pipe bands in the march.

A short time prior to the planned opening ceremonies, Michael MacNeil's family lived in Cape Breton. However, his father, who had worked in No. 1 Colliery in Sydney Mines, had his leg crushed in a mining accident. After that

the family, like many other islanders, was forced to leave their home to find work in Ontario.

*Fifteen-year-old Michael MacNeil on the Causeway two days before the official ceremonies.*

## "A CASE OF CAPE BRETON SPITE"

The links between Cape Breton and its nomadic offspring are strong, and when my parents learned of the Causeway's opening celebrations, they made plans to go back home for a vacation and, while there, to take in the ceremonies. Around this time, my parents heard that the opening was to feature one hundred pipers from various walks of life. My mother wrote the "powers at hand" at the time and requested that I be allowed to march with the one hundred but I was refused based on the prerequisite that all of the pipers had to be residents of the province.

When my father, Mike Senior, heard the committee's decision he was so upset he decided to take matters in his own hands. Being refused by some bureaucrats wasn't going to deter him. Dad was bound and bent I was going to march across, playing my pipes, with or without permission, and he had a plan. As the family car reached the mainland side of the Causeway on the Thursday, August 11, before the Saturday opening, my father had me change into a white shirt and a Bruce tartan kilt. It was a beautiful evening, the kind where the sky looked like a child had emptied her box of yellow crayons in order to create the right amount of gold streaks and when she ran out of yellow, she tipped each long stroke with splashes of vivid orange. On the mainland side of the Causeway Dad stopped the car and had me march all the way across, playing all the while. I know I played "The Road to the Isles" over the bridge and I never stopped until I reached the Cape Breton side.

I guess it gave my father and mother immeasurable satisfaction to see me march across. However as August 13, 1955, the official day for the celebrations neared, not everyone was happy with the idea of becoming connected to the mainland. One of the things that I remember was when I was at my grandmother's house, and she was asked if she wanted to go with the rest of the family to the opening. She replied, "Why would I want to go and mix with those heathens on the other side?" She stayed home by herself and the rest of us went to the opening. We enjoyed the day and the music with the "heathens."
—Michael MacNeil

Jim MacDonnell from Inverness tells of playing with the Inverness Pipe Band and crossing the Causeway the day before the official opening in order for the National Film Board to film the end of a story they'd been working on for eight weeks that summer. Although *The Wandering Piper* appears to have disappeared without a trace from the records of the NFB, the film was shot in and around the village of Deepdale, Cape Breton, a coal-mining town. The cameraman for the film was Johnny Foster and the soundman was Frank Oben. Filming took place the summer of 1955 when Jim was ten. The entire neighbourhood was involved in the taping and the film included a Christmas scene in July.

## "TOO SMALL TO HOLD THE PIPES"

In the opening scene of the film two young boys are fishing back of the racetrack when we hear the skirl of the pipes. This is when Sandy Boyd made his first appearance, playing as he went. The wandering minstrel turns out to be a world champion who had trained under another champion, John McColl. He stayed in the village two years teaching the men and boys how to play the pipes.

When it drew near time for the Inverness Band to play in the opening, I wasn't going to be able to participate because my older brother, Harold, was using the only set of pipes available. In the film, the neighbourhood banded together, raising money and collecting funds so I could play the pipes at the opening. The film ends with the neighbours buying me the pipes, but really the National Film Board bought my pipes. The only problem was they were a full-sized set and I had to play with my head in between the bass and the tenor drone to keep the pipes from sliding off my shoulder. Both my brother and I wore the MacPherson tartan kilt, white tunics and spats all made by our mother.
—Jim MacDonnell

Blisters forming on heels and sweltering under their kilts, the pipers illustrated the lengths they would go to have their music heard and to be part of the history of such a memorable event. Jim MacDonnell also recalls that, "Pipe instructor, Sandy Boyd, proudly marched across the full length of the Causeway never missing a step but when he reached the other side he said to his buddy, 'My foot hurts.' On closer examination he realized he'd walked the length of the Causeway with a tack in his foot."

When Sandra (Rose) Boutquin was a child, she wanted to play the fiddle, but her mother wanted her to play pipes. Her mother won. Sandra is currently playing with Hamilton Police Pipe Band—2004 Canadian and North American champions—and will be travelling to Scotland to compete at the World Championships in Glasgow in 2005.

Although Sandra didn't fully comprehend the significance of her historic march across the causeway, she is very proud to say that she was part of the MacDonald Hundred Pipe Band at the opening ceremonies.

Pipe bands playing at the opening ceremonies.

## "BLISTERS AND BILE"

In August 13, 1955, I was an eager nine-year-old. The previous fall, my mother signed me up for piping lessons with the MacDonald Hundred Pipe Band, created by A. W. R. MacKenzie. Our band was one of the bands playing across the Causeway and it was quite a feather in one's cap to be chosen to play. Since I was only nine and still on practice chanter, I was picked to carry the Nova Scotia flag and march with the band on that special day.

What a day it was! Hot, windy, dusty, but exciting! I lived in North Sydney and it seemed like it took my mother, my two aunts and me about five or six hours to get to the Causeway from home. Of course, the roads were not paved and were strewn with rocks, big and small. I got car sick as I always did in those days, and I'm sure we had to stop my Aunt Nina's 1951 green Anglia about a dozen times so I could throw up.

I remember the crowds—to me it seemed like the whole world was there. Someone pointed out the premier—I thought that he was akin to God.

Finally after what seemed like hours, and probably was, the parade started off. The MacDonald Hundred played only two tunes all the way across; "The Hundred Pipers" and "The Road to the Isles." It must have been so boring for the pip-ers and drummers. Heavy woollen kilts, black velvet tunics and plaids weighed us down and raised our body temperatures about ten degrees.

After what seemed like an eternity, the parade was over. My feet were blistered; I was exhausted, hot, cranky and unfortunately in no state to properly appreciate the importance of the day. About a month later, I received a certificate stating that I had done the Causeway march. It had a beautiful Nova Scotia tartan ribbon and I soon learned to cherish it and understand that I had played a part, a tiny part, in an event that would go down in Nova Scotia's history.
—Sandra Boutquin

After being told the Inverness County Band would lead the parade, then being told they wouldn't, the band master, John Kennedy, a much-decorated piper, went to great lengths to make sure one of his own band was at the head of the procession.

## "WHO LED THE PARADE?"

Our band was the only one from Inverness County, where the Causeway is situated, so I decided to appoint Al Skinner, a drum major from Inverness, to lead the band—only to learn there would be six or seven other drum majors in attendance on opening day. It crossed my mind to get some flag-bearers to lead the march, but first I had to get flags and kilts for the flag-bearers. I knew the Boy Scouts had a Union Jack and a flagpole at St. Matthew's Church in Inverness, so I approached the minister and asked him if we could borrow the flag. I knew there was a Nova Scotia flag at the Belmont Hotel in Margaree Forks, a distance of about eighteen miles. I had Al Skinner drive me there and we borrowed that flag from the proprietor.

My next obstacle was the acquisition of two uniforms for the flag-bearers. My mother bought a kilt from an ex-soldier, and I borrowed the second one from a shop outside of town. Next I asked my brother-in-law, Charles MacArthur, and another friend, Earl Smith, if they would do the honours. They both agreed. They were six footers and looked good in their uniforms. They both wore the army tunics they had worn overseas during World War Two.
—John Kennedy

Pipe Major George Dey from 36th Heavy Anti-Aircraft (Reserve) Pipe Band in Halifax and formerly from Dundee, Scotland, was asked to be the senior pipe major; however, the Cape Breton Regiment wanted Pipe Major (Black Jack) MacDonald to lead the mass bands. George Dey was the official tuner for Peter Henderson Bagpipes Co. in Scotland until he left to come to Canada in 1906.

Pipe Corporal Joe Tummonds said, "No one could tune pipes like Pipe Major Dey, so the compromise was that Dey tuned all the pipers' pipes and Black Jack and the Cape Breton highlanders led the parade."

Other bands that participated in the Causeway crossing were the 63rd Halifax Rifles Pipe Band, 219 New Glasgow Royal Canadian Army Cadet Corps Pipes and Drum, Antigonish Highland Society Pipe Band, Inverness County Pipe Band, Cape Breton Highland Pipe Band, Halifax Naval Pipe Band, Essex Scottish (New Brunswick), HMCS Cape Breton Pipe Band, Mabou Ceilidh Pipe Band, and Cape Breton Celtic Society Pipe Band. Months before the event the bands received the tunes: "The Hundred Pipers," "The Road to the Isles," "Green Hills" and "The Battle's Over." These were simple tunes, but the organizers of the event wanted all of the pipers to play the tunes in the same setting.

Edna Phelan, who watched the opening ceremonies from her trailer on the top of the hill overlooking the work site, said, "The sound of the pipers coming over the Causeway was out of this world." Phelan's husband was a construction worker.

David Betts, piper and resident of Dorset, England, remembers the tunes played for the opening of the Causeway weren't as tuneful as the pipers had planned them to be.

## "NAME THAT TUNE"

In the summer of 1955, I was a young bagpiper with the Halifax Rifles militia and as such was chosen as one of the official "one hundred pipers" to play at the Causeway opening. We travelled by coach from Halifax to the mainland side of the Causeway and were formed up and fed in a wooded, hilly area a mile or so away, along with other bands from all over Cape Breton and the mainland. After much tuning of drones and checking of boots and uniforms, our band, which, as I recall, consisted of eight pipers and three or four drummers, was assigned our position in the ranks, and all went well as we marched down out of the hills in the bright sunshine, playing some stirring tunes.

We formed up at the end of the Causeway and stood silently in the scorching heat while the dignitaries assembled. To this day I remain heartily grateful to our pipe sergeant, Alan Cant, who had given us permission to leave our tunics in the coach and parade in shirtsleeves. August 13 was truly baking hot, and I felt sorry for the fellows around me from other bands sweating in their heavy and scratchy tunics as the ceremonies got under way and seemed to us, standing in the sun, to go on for an uncomfortably long time.

Finally the orders came from the front, "By the left, quick march!" and a short time later "Pipes up!" For the uninitiated, this is the signal for pipers to shoulder their drones and silently inflate the pipe-bags with air from their lungs, ready for the first note. Listening to the thump of the drums from the rear, we marched along the Causeway, watching for the start signal from the parade pipe major. When he smartly lowered his staff, all one hundred official pipers, plus a few dozen more at the rear of the column, all snapped our elbows onto our pipe-bags in unison and started playing simultaneously.

This of course was what was meant to happen. What was NOT meant to happen was that half the band started playing "The Hundred Pipers" and the other half "The Road to the Isles"! Up to that point all arrangements had been efficiently organized and carried out in true military fashion, but someone, somewhere had forgotten one small, important detail: to call out to the bandsmen the name of the tune. If I recall correctly, all these years later, we in the Halifax Rifles contingent had been told that the start-off tune would be "The Hundred Pipers" and that we would play "The Road to the Isles" later on after the speeches and ribbon-cutting. But comparing notes with other bands that afternoon we learned that some of them had been told just the opposite.

As we crossed the causeway there was cacophony—at least to a piper's ears. An individual piper, thinking he was playing the correct "Road" tune, would hear others around him playing "Hundred." So he and others in his own group would switch. But then other bands or individuals nearby, fearing THEY were at fault, would switch from "Hundred" to "Road." I remember seeing pipers up and down the ranks asking each other what they were playing, some people even looking back and frowning reprovingly at those behind. We hoped the spectators along the sides of the Causeway were all tone deaf and unaware of the eccentric mixture of sounds we were producing.

Eventually we got ourselves sorted out, and by the time we reached the reviewing stand where the guest speakers, photographers, and the main body of onlookers were crowded together we were all in perfect harmony playing the same tune, "The Road to the Isles"...or was it "The Hundred Pipers"?

Pipe Corporal Joseph Albert Tummonds, now living in British Columbia, said of the event, "In my life I have accomplished many things but I cherish this certificate as I know that some fifty years later there will not be many of them around." Joe played with the 36th Heavy Anti-Aircraft Regiment Pipe Band from Halifax and is still a very active piper. He has piped in competition all over Canada and Scotland.
—David Betts

*Joe Tummonds (left), with his friend Bill Fisher, had to march in full uniform despite the heat.*

To this day, piping is still part of the tradition of crossing the Causeway. Summer tourists who come to the island are greeted at the tourist bureau on the Cape Breton side of the Causeway by a piper. Carleen MacDonald spent one summer playing the pipes in this very way.

## "QUESTIONS ASKED THE PIPER"

*Carleen MacDonald welcoming visitors to Cape Breton at the Tourist Bureau near the Causeway.*

L et's see...what to say about my piping? Well, I have to be honest—I didn't pipe only for the sake of enjoyment. Luckily, that talent helped pay my way through university. Even though the job could be very tiresome, it was still better than many other summer jobs that my friends had to take, and at least I was able to get in lots of practice! The outfit was uncomfortable on very hot days, but it was a necessity, as most tourists would not have appreciated a plain-clothes piper quite as much. I remember some of the tourists didn't like my sunglasses, saying they clashed with the kilt, but they too were a necessity for me as I get a headache if I'm squinting in the sun.

What questions did the tourists ask? Well, you name it and they asked it! I suppose the most popular question was, "How does that [the pipes] work?" This, of course, requires a comprehensive answer, as the bagpipes are a very compli-cated instrument. I was able to create a simple response; I would usually show people what the reeds look like (both the drone reeds and the chanter one) and explain how the air flows through the bag and hence through the reeds to create the sound. I would also have to point out that the three drones that lay on my shoulder made the background hum, while I sounded out the melody using the chanter (playing notes in a way similar to playing a recorder).

They would also ask about the tartan in my kilt. I wore the Royal Stewart tartan, as that was the kilt my pipe band wore. I would always point out that my hat badge was my family's clan, Clad Ranald. Tourists also wanted to know the purpose of my "purse" (the sporran). Unfortunately, I didn't own a flask to carry in it as other pipers do, but the tourists would get a laugh when I showed them what I kept in there: usually a comb and bobby pins, sometimes some money or sunscreen! I guess they were hoping for more traditional items. Also, they very often noticed my *sqian dubh*. This was the small dagger I kept in my sock. Again, it was really more for show than anything else (mine was as dull as a butter knife), but tourists liked the idea that in battle Scots would have used such an instrument. I guess because the pipes are something so strange to many tourists, a lot would ask me if I was making the music up as I went along. I would have to explain to them that I was playing actual melodies I had learned and memorized. Also, there were usually requests for "That song pipers play." Many didn't know the name, but were usually referring to "Scotland the Brave." Also, "Amazing Grace" was requested quite a bit. And then there were some tourists who would cover their ears or say that they thought "the squealing" was awful. I didn't take it personally—not everyone can have an appreciation for things Scottish.

And then there was the silly question, "What are you wearing under your kilt?" My former employer from Margaree, John May, told me the best answer to that question: "Shoes and socks!"

As to why it was important to pipe at the Causeway, I guess I wanted to pipe there because so many people say that the one thing they remember about visiting Cape Breton was the piper playing as they crossed the Causeway.
—Carleen MacDonald

MEMORIES OF THE OPENING
Billy Joe MacLean, presently the mayor of Port Hawkesbury, was nineteen when the Causeway opened in August 1955 and even back then, he was trying to figure out how he could turn such a gathering into a way of making some money. According to the story he told Mary Ellen MacIntyre in the *Mail Star*, he found a pile of plastic licence plate attachments that read "Welcome to Cape Breton Highlands" in his uncle's basement, which he bought from his uncle for twenty-two cents apiece. On the day of the opening, MacLean hired another fellow to sell his product for a dollar apiece while he spent the day selling hot dogs to the crowds. He said, "I sold every damn hot dog and plastic thing I had and came away with $2,600 for a day's work."

Safety and crowd control were two key issues for the RCMP on opening day when an estimated 40,000 people gathered at the water's edge to celebrate. Officers like Corporal Maurice Morrow and Constables Eugene

Constable Donald MacIntosh was on duty near the swing bridge the day of the opening.

Pendergast and Donald MacIntosh were three of those who served. Constable MacIntosh's duties included escorting the commanding officer, J. S. Henry, and the head radio technician Don MacNeil from Sydney. For the remainder of his time on duty he was posted to crowd control on the west end of the swing bridge. (Unbeknownst to him, his future wife, Dorothy Baillieul, resident of Port Hawkesbury and secretary for Harry MacKenzie, was part of this crowd.) MacIntosh said, "My biggest challenge was keeping people from climbing up on the bridge so they could see the ceremonies better. I was afraid some of them would end up in the canal."

Constable Eugene (Casey) Pendergast, part of the Truro detachment of RCMP, was another of the escorting members of the RCMP who led people across the Causeway at the opening ceremonies on a motorcycle. While carrying out his duties, David C. Macneill from Halifax hailed him and asked him to escort a doctor to the aid of an executive from the Halifax Trust Company who was in need of urgent medical attention. Later Pendergast received a letter of thanks and high praise from Mr. Macneill. The letter stated, "The handling of the heavy traffic was, in the opinion of the writer, that of an expert and his courtesy and kindness was much appreciated."

On the day of the opening, Isobel Harling and her husband, Ellsworth, joined the dignitaries and walked across the Causeway behind the one hundred pipers. Later the O. J. McCulloch Company held a big party in Mulgrave for their workers and the whole town was invited to celebrate the grand opening. Harling further explained her husband's role with the project. "I was a new mother with a three-month-old son and my husband, Ellsworth Harling, was an engineer for O. J. McCulloch Limited when we moved to Mulgrave. Harry MacKenzie, chief engineer for the same firm, and his wife also lived in Mulgrave during the construction of the Causeway. We both had to learn to be content in our tiny makeshift trailers and make a home in a town of 1500 people, many of whom were connected to the railway and the ferries and resented the arrival of the 'come from aways' who would work to build a causeway, then leave their town poor and deserted.

"I watched the changes in the community when four hundred single construction workers rolled into town but there was one important difference between me and the locals: I had the advantage of knowing someday I would move on while the locals had no such hope.

"During the construction my husband would take me to see the site and it was fascinating watching them dig the tunnels into the mountain and put the dynamite inside for the blasts. The man who was in charge of the blasting project was from British Columbia and he earned the nickname of 'Hardrock Shannon.' Every time I went to the site and watched the large trucks dump their loads of fill into the Strait I wanted to ask one question; in fact I'd still like to ask it. I'd like someone to explain to me how the rocks are held together."

Despite the best-laid plans, organizers of major events often overlook the obvious, with often humourous results. On the day of the opening, Bernie MacDonald witnessed the near-catastrophe of arriving dignitaries getting dunked in the Strait.

## "THE DIGNITARIES HAD WET FEET"

During the pre-opening days of the Canso Causeway, before activities began for the big day, there was a small stone-crushing and trucking operation in progress in the area. This non-causeway related activity involved a gravel-

*Ellsworth Harling and his son, David, in 1955.*

*An inspection tour of the new causeway.*

crushing operation near Havre Boucher and the trucking of the crushed stone to a stockpile in Aulds Cove just off the Causeway roadbed where it turns left across the Strait. My job was the weighing of the trucks at the platform scale-house before they dumped their load and returned to the crusher in Havre Boucher.

My location in the scale house was an ideal spot from which to observe the preparatory activities taking place for the big day. One of these activities was happening just behind the scale house: the construction of a temporary "floating dock" for those dignitaries who would arrive by water. This dock was located at the edge of the water on the Mulgrave side of the Causeway just where the Causeway turned to cross the Strait. The dock was simple and temporary, consisting of several empty fifty-five gallon oil drums for flotation, on top of which was constructed a wooden platform. From this floating dock, a small wooden footbridge led across some open water to a wooden stairway, which in turn provided a means of climbing over the large boulders that lined the side of the Causeway.

As the big day approached, supervisors carried out many inspections of this floating dock structure. On the day before the opening ceremonies the Royal Canadian Navy actually arrived in a thirty-foot launch to check out the

approach, the location, and the water depth, and to do a practice run before the transporting and landing of naval officials and other dignitaries. This indeed was an impressive sight to watch as the seamen manoeuvred their launch up to and away from the floating dock with great precision and timing.

When the big day finally arrived, I was one of only a few who knew of this point of landing, so I watched with keen interest. As the time approached for the arrival of visiting dignitaries, I noted that for the first time everyone who had previously come individually to check out the dock had now all arrived at the same time. As fate would have it, someone must have underestimated the number of people the floating dock could hold, though all appeared to be going well until the arrival of the naval launch. The launch approached, the receiving line moved out onto the floating dock, the advance party of seamen stepped off the launch and onto the floating dock. The additional weight was more than the dock could support, and the dock began to sink.

Nobody seemed to notice the dock's slow submersion until several people got their feet wet; some were in the water up to their knees before the scrambling started. At this point the seamen jumped back onto the launch and most of those on the dock ran for the stairs.

Within several seconds the dock was floating normally again, and with fewer people on the dock, this time everyone arrived safely at the ceremonies. Except for some embarrassment on the part of the authorities, nobody seemed the worse for it, although some went through the ceremonies with wet feet and pants, doing their best to keep a serious face.
—Bernie MacDonald

Marilyn Manthorne MacPhee, now living in Port Williams about five kilometres from her husband's family home, was only a young girl when she travelled with her family to watch the opening ceremonies at the Causeway.

## "A FAMILY EVENT"

The opening of the Canso Causeway was an important event in the life of my family. I grew up in Seal Harbour, on the eastern shore of Guysborough County, one of three daughters of Bernie and Lillian Manthorne. Until 1951, my father had fished from our little village cove in his Cape Island boat. That year he gave up fishing to find a more lucrative way of supporting his family. He spent some months crewing on a coal-hauling ship on the Great Lakes.

In the spring of 1953, he joined the wholesale grocer firm of Johnson and MacDonald Ltd. headquartered in New Glasgow. His job was that of a travelling salesman. His territory consisted of the eastern parts of Antigonish and Guysborough Counties and on alternate weeks, Inverness County. He took orders for groceries from small stores in towns and villages in these counties until he retired in 1977.

Each weekend when he arrived home, he filled our heads with stories of his travels. When he came from Cape Breton, he talked of the huge amounts of rock blasted from Cape Porcupine and hauled by gigantic trucks to be dumped into the Canso Strait. He told of lives lost during the construction of the Causeway. He was really looking forward to its completion so that he wouldn't have to spend precious time waiting for the car ferry that crossed from Mulgrave to Port Hawkesbury.

On the day of the official opening I was excited. This occasion so far from home meant that we would drive to a paved highway and travel on it for some distance before reaching our destination. Also, I was still getting used to the idea of our family owning a car. So, that morning our family—my mom, dad, two sisters, granddad and I—set off in a blue 1954 Dodge. We drove to Guysborough town and on to Manchester where we followed the shore through Port Shoreham to Mulgrave. We parked near Cape Porcupine and watched the

*Some of the crowds that caused Dr. MacMillan to miss a delivery.*

festivities from the top of the Cape. On
that day, there were more people than
I had ever seen in my life. It was also
the first time I had ever seen or heard
a bagpiper, let alone so many of them.
—Marilyn MacPhee

Although other people were gathering to
celebrate the official opening of the Canso
Causeway, August 13, 1955 posed a problem
for Dr. C. Lamont MacMillan of Baddeck.
The doctor wanted to attend the ceremony,
but leaving his practice would mean there
would be no one to cover for him in the event
of an emergency. As a Cape Breton MLA,
and having lived through many arguments
and criticisms levied by a number of citizens
while the Causeway was being constructed,
Dr. MacMillan had a special interest in attending the celebrations. To solve his dilemma
he called on Dr. Myers, a cardiologist and
specialist in internal medicine with a practice
in Washington, DC, who was staying in the
family's summer home at Beinn Breagh. Dr.
Myers was married to a granddaughter of
Professor Alexander Graham Bell.

In his book, *Memoirs of a Cape Breton Doctor*, Dr. MacMillan writes, "My wife was all
ready for the trip, fuming because up to this
point I had not said whether or not I would
be able to go. Finally I decided to go, and once
I had made up my mind, we weren't long in
getting on the road. The ribbon was to be cut
at two o'clock."

By the time the doctor and his wife arrived
at the Strait, the crowds were so large that it
was impossible for find a parking spot where
he could make a quick getaway should an
emergency arise. Fortunately, the baby daughter born to Mrs. Aloysius MacKinnon of Iona
during his absence was well-attended by two
prominent doctors, Dr. Myers and his col-
league, Dr. D. Jarmen, also from Washington,
DC. After his return, Dr. MacMillan learned
that neither of the doctors had attended a
delivery since their intern years. Dr. MacMillan wrote, "But they had a perfect patient and
everything went along well. The baby was
born shortly before two o'clock. The doctors
watched the clock on the wall, and exactly at
two, just as the ribbon was to be cut on the
Causeway, they cut the cord!"

It was said Mrs. MacKinnon was pleased
with the doctors' work for she named the new
baby girl Jarmine Myra, in honour of both of
them.

*The car ferry John Cabot in 1952, after being hit by the freighter Canadian Victor. The Cabot burned at its dock in May 1955.*

# CHAPTER 5

# IMPACT OF THE CAUSEWAY

Before the Canso Causeway was built, the Strait of Canso was considered a formidable barrier and those wanting to cross it were left to the inadequacies of the connecting train and ferry system of the day. Cape Breton Island thrusts out into the North Atlantic and the rugged outline of its land mass has been shaped and re-shaped by the ocean's savage currents, which are caused by ever-changing wind patterns and what Cape Bretoners call "The Big Ice" drifting down on the Labrador currents.

Winter conditions prior to 1955 found the Strait ice-clogged. The ice coupled with high winds whipped up during storms made ferry crossings dangerous, and the long delays hindered the island's economy. Although the construction of the Causeway did benefit industrial Cape Breton, in that the new link allowed coal and steel from this area to be moved to their markets more efficiently, it was devastating to the Strait area. Mulgrave, Port Hawkesbury and Point Tupper had a combined population of about 2,500 people and approximately 450 obtained their living from the ferry system. Whole families were separated as a result of major job losses when the John Cabot discontinued its ferry service between Mulgrave and Port Hawkesbury and the Scotia ferries and railway yards discontinued their operations in Mulgrave and Point Tupper. Railway servicing facilities were also removed from Havre Boucher, Mulgrave, Point Tupper, and other points bordering the Strait. In May of 1955, CNR estimated 334 of their employees were put out of work when the last train pulled out of Point Tupper, the last ferry crossed the Strait, and their facilities closed. "I can't see anything but a ghost town here unless we get some other industry," said veteran railwayman Elmer Oliver, who was in charge of the CNR yard at Point Tupper. (Elmer worked for the CNR from approximately 1915 to 1956. He moved to Yarmouth for a year after the Scotia ferry shut down.)

Today, there's hardly a trace of the village of Point Tupper. The once-vibrant community has been levelled in favour of industry. Former residents express a sense of loss and refer to their missing identity. They can no longer show their children and grandchildren the place where they once lived, worked and played. Although Mulgrave has survived, many of the residents still express remorse and say their community has been lost to them. Previous to the Causeway's completion both communities boasted everything a flourishing community could provide. The sound of train-wheels clattering day and night was music to their ears.

"They studied the rock but they didn't know anything about what was going to happen to the people," said Leonard O'Neil, mayor of Mulgrave during the Causeway construction period. O'Neil also suffered from the changes: after the Causeway was completed the sheriff came knocking at the door of his car dealership. O'Neil lost his business and had to travel to Halifax to find work.

Since 1955 the economy of the Strait area, like the tide, has ebbed and flowed. The Causeway's completion brought both hope for a brighter future, with the promise of new industry coming to the area, and despair as a way of life ended when the trains and ferries stopped moving across the Strait. The arrival of the Causeway did bring one obvious benefit: it stopped the ice from flowing through the Strait on the north side and as a result, the south side became an ice-free port. Gradually, through the leadership and efforts of the Four Counties Development Association, which promoted the ice-free port and its capability of servicing the world's largest super tankers, several industries were enticed to move to the area. Stora Kopparberg of Sweden built Nova Scotia Forest Industries, a major pulp mill, in Point Tupper, followed by a paper mill. The new port attracted Gulf Oil to build a refinery and a deep-water marine terminal, Atomic Energy of Canada built a heavy water plant, Nova Scotia Power built a generating station and Georgia Pacific built a gypsum-processing plant in the late 1950s and early 1960s. Despite these businesses leaving the community, in 2002 nearly seventeen million metric tonnes of cargo was loaded or discharged from Statia Terminals and other stations in the area. Today the Canso Strait is the fourth busiest port in Canada based on tonnage of product shipped. Of course it is hard to know what might have resulted from different decisions, but had a bridge been built instead of a causeway, there would have been no ice-free port, and the southwest end of the Island may not have developed to the extent it has today. Indeed, Port Hawkesbury's mayor, Billy Joe MacLean, predicts the town will grow so fast that in ten years it will be a city.

Joyce Oliver-Snair is part of the committee formed to celebrate the Canso Causeway's fiftieth anniversary. Having been born after the Causeway's completion, Oliver-Snair says she knows nothing of the ferries, but she does know of the results of the Causeway.

## "DOWN THE ROAD"

In 1954, Elmer Oliver posed proudly for a photo that would appear in the

Saturday edition of the Cape Breton Standard, along with "Doom Towns," a feature on what the completion of the Canso Causeway would mean to Point Tupper, Port Hawkesbury, and Mulgrave. A railway man, Elmer worked the Scotia run from Point Tupper to Mulgrave all his life, and its approaching end caused him great worry for the futures of his family, friends and neighbours. He felt that unless some other industry came to Point Tupper, the community would die.

In 1955, Elmer's son, Harold Oliver, was called by his superiors to go and throw the switch for the first train to cross the newly completed causeway. After completing the task, he returned to work with no fanfare. Unlike his father, he was not prepared to wait for the photo op; in his words, he had "just knocked a lot of men out of work with that single turn of the switch," including his own father. In his mind, it was nothing to be proud of.

I am the daughter and granddaughter of Harold and Elmer. Elmer wished for more industry for the people thrown out of work, and Point Tupper got it. But the price was high. Point Tupper of the 50s and 60s is gone; not just the people, but the homes and landscape that we knew as children. Gone is the "Lane," the "Y"—even the road has been changed. In its place stand cold, steel buildings, and

Elmer Oliver

Harold Oliver

only a hint of the rail that brought life to the community in the years leading up to the opening of the Causeway. But the sense of community still remains strong among local families as well as among those who went "down the road."

Today the Causeway takes me to work every day in Mulgrave, where I celebrate with that community its survival. Although Elmer and Harold are both gone, the industry that changed the Point Tupper of my childhood provided my father and now my husband with employment so they could raise their families here. We have come full circle, but most importantly the Causeway has become the sign for my family "from away" that they are "home," truly something that needs to be celebrated. —Joyce Oliver-Snair

Mel Joseph Purcell, one of eight children of James and Hattie Purcell, was born in Mulgrave in 1931. Mel attended school in Mulgrave and continued his education in Quebec, where he became a schoolteacher and later a principal. From his home in Longueil, Quebec, where he is now retired and lives with his family, Mel writes fondly of the Mulgrave of Yesterday.

## MULGRAVE OF YESTERDAY
### MEL PURCELL

There's a town I know called Mulgrave, a town down by the sea,
Just off the wide Atlantic, where the tides are running free,
It's on the Strait of Canso, and through the summer's days,
A strait that tends to turquoise blue, with whitecaps in its ways.
The town lies on an uprise, that slopes a mile or more,
And looks off to its sister town along the other shore.
It used to be a railway town before the causeway came,
But now it stands off to the side, and hardly knows its name.
But back there in its "heyday" when it was in the race,
It was an active centre then, a busy, well-known place.

The townsmen worked at everything a railway could provide,
From shunting cars around the yard to "icing" on the side.

The train wheels clattered day and night with hardly any lull,
With the Scotia steaming back and forth on never-resting hull.
Boats came in from towns around, in sizes small and great,
To meet the trains from day to day, and pick up mail and freight.
The fish plant thrived on staple cod that streamed in from the Banks,
And now and then strange boats appeared for fuel at Irving's tanks.
The ferryboats down by the cove, made trips at steady pace,
And locals on a nearby bank took in each car and face.

The restaurants were the Sweetshop and Tip Top farther down,
And grocery stores were everywhere and movies came to town.
The sidewalk was a busy place, as few then owned a car,
And women took their babies out in strollers, near and far.
The children all kept ready smiles, and money was unknown,
And considered it a "rare old treat," to have an ice-cream cone.
On top of this, the nicest thing was people's frame of mind,
As everyone was happier, and no one was unkind,
And everybody laughed a lot, in going to and fro,
And stopped to chat or tell a joke, or yell a big "hello."
But that's the town of yesterday, the town it used to be,
My childhood town of Mulgrave, the one that's lost to me.

## THE FERRY WORKERS

At exactly one minute to midnight on the same day the last CN ferry crossed the Strait of Canso, the following notice went out to the men working on the ferries and the railway: "As a result of the commencement of train service across the Causeway, our Strait of Canso Ferry Service will be discontinued at 11:59 P.M. May 14, 1955. I am obliged therefore to notify you that your employment with the Canadian National Railways will terminate at the close of business on the said date. It is regretted that at the said time there is no other work with the railway which can be offered you."

On September 29, 1955, CNR completed a two-day survey of the industrial potential of the Strait. The communities near the Canso Causeway, especially Point Tupper and Mulgrave, were becoming ghost towns. The survey reported seventy-five heads of families in Mulgrave had been on unemployment insurance since May 14 of that year. Several months later many of the men still hadn't found work, and families were beginning to leave Mulgrave. Earlier it had been rumoured that three pulp and paper mills were interested in coming to the area and harvesting the 600,000 cords of wood available. In the early fall, Mulgrave was optimistic the mill would be situated on the mainland side of the Strait, but this never happened. The December headlines of the Victoria–Inverness Bulletin read: "Away from home, but employed." These were the reported words of Frank O'Neil, who until the Scotia II made its last run on May 14 of that year had been the skipper on the train ferry. After the ferry's last run he and forty-three other former crew members of the ferry system were without work. Following twenty-six years of service, O'Neil and six other former CNR employees left the area to take jobs with the new freighter-ferry, the Bluenose, on the Yarmouth-Bar Harbour run. The veterans leaving were Frank O'Neil, Alphonsus and Eugene O'Neil, Xavier Keating, William Keating, Alex Murray and Oscar Hadley.

## "LEAVING HOME"

I was a Centennial Project baby (born in 1967 at St. Martha's hospital in Antigonish), so I have never known the Strait of Canso without the Causeway. My life, however, is inextricably linked with both the Strait of Canso and the Causeway.

My late paternal grandfather, Edward Carter, my paternal uncle Robert Alexander Carter, and my father, Joseph Edward Carter, all worked upon the CN rail ferries, the Scotias that ran from Mulgrave to Point Tupper up to 1955. My dad's family were ferry workers and fishermen. The Causeway ended life as his family knew it, stopping the ferries from the west as well as the lobsters and fish from the north.

The year 2005 will see the fiftieth anniversary of the migration of my dad's entire family from Hadleyville in the District of Guysborough to the town of Yarmouth where they found work on the old CN ferry MV *Bluenose* that ran from Yarmouth to Bar Harbour, Maine. My Dad did not migrate with his family, choosing to stay on his mother's family's Loyalist homestead along the shore of Chedabuctou Bay in Hadleyville. His brother and most of his sisters still live in Yarmouth, visiting their homeland in Hadleyville once or twice a year.

You can see that the building of the Canso Causeway has had a major impact on my dad's family, scattering it across Nova Scotia from the lands of their ancestors. It has also had a huge impact on mine, for I am half a Caper.

My mother, Anne Christine Carter (nee Fraser), is the daughter of Bill Fraser and the late Kay Fraser from Port Hastings, Inverness County. My mom spent most of her working life, from the age of seventeen to her retirement in the late 1990s, as a schoolteacher in Guysborough County and still lives with my dad in their home in Hadleyville. My dad spent eight years commuting across the Canso Causeway to work at the pulp mill in Point Tupper that has gone by the various names of NSFP, Stora, Stora-Kopparberg, and Stora-Enso.

So, as you can see, the Canso Causeway has had a huge impact on my very existence. The Causeway destroyed my paternal grandfather's family, just as it made mine. —Sean Carter

Although a causeway was considered necessary for development and progress, fishermen and naturalists are among the many who still debate its benefits. As early as November 1955, a note in the Victoria–Inverness Bulletin confirmed that underwater marine species were confused as a result of discovering a causeway in their path of navigation. During a northeast gale, thousands of bill fish were dashed against the rocks and spewed across the roadway.

The fishermen who travelled through the Strait of Canso to go to their fishing grounds along the north shore lost wages during the final stages of the Causeway's construction. Many were angry because they had not been consulted on how the construction would affect their livelihood, while others were convinced the link disturbed the flow of lobster larvae through the Strait. Still others believed the Causeway upset the route of the migrating herring.

Keith Guptill, once named "high line fisherman" for the Port of Canso for the years 1951 to 1960, fished in the Marilyn Ann out of his home port of Canso. He confirmed the disruption caused by the opening of the Causeway: "During the last year of construction, they closed the passageway through the Strait and we had to use the Bras D'Or Lake in order to get to our fishing grounds." He went on to say that a typical trip through the Strait of Canso to his usual fishing grounds around Port Hood Island and up to Cheticamp normally took him eighteen to twenty-two hours. A trip to another good fishing area, the region between Cape Jack near Havre Boucher and Cape George, near Antigonish, took about twelve hours. "Once the Strait was closed, the trip up through the Bras d'Or added ten hours to sixteen hours to the round trip."

Not only were Guptill and others inconvenienced by the length of time it took to make the trip through the Bras d'Or lake, but it was treacherous. The numerous islands scattered through the lake made travel by boat at night risky. Guptill remembers helping to take another fisherman off the mud: "He'd gone down through the islands in the daylight but the shadows had fooled him and he went aground with a full load on." The longer hours needed to get to the fishing grounds coupled with the necessity of navigating the lake during the daylight hours meant fishermen lost their best time to catch haddock, a more lucrative product. "We could fish flounder in the dark but they only brought us three cents a pound," says Guptill. "Haddock brought us five cents a pound but they swam in deeper waters and we needed the daylight to catch them." As a result, the return trip cut into their fishing times and reduced their wages by fifteen to twenty per cent. Guptill's own earnings ranged from $3,500 to $4,800 per year.

## "A FISHERMAN'S STORY"

I eased the throttle to idle and disengaged the clutch of the wheel-house-controlled diesel engine before coming slowly to a standstill on the glassy waters of the Strait of Canso. The cliffs of Cape Porcupine were above me, and a voice on the radio telephone informed me of the latest weather forecast from the Canadian Fishermen's Broadcast.

As I listened to the announcer go through the preliminaries and the weather synopsis, I studied the scarred face of the Cape a few hundred yards off the port side. Man had done the impossible by blasting huge pieces of stone from the face of the cliff to build a causeway across the deep gorge that separated Cape Breton Island from the mainland of Nova Scotia. I thought of how the waters of the great Atlantic had flowed unmolested through this Strait for centuries and of the fish that went north and south in their season from Chedabucto Bay and the Atlantic on the south side to George's Bay and the Gulf of St. Lawrence on the north side, and wondered how this dam that man was building would affect my future as captain of a fifty-six-foot fishing dragger. My thoughts were interrupted by the voice of the announcer as he finally got around to the weather report for the Northumberland Strait and the Gulf of

St. Lawrence. "Light winds increasing to north-east fifteen miles and snow," the announcer said. Under different circumstances I would have been pleased with the report, but now it only served to increase the uneasiness that I had felt for the last two days, especially since we had left Canso three hours earlier.

Now that I had the weather information, I snapped the receiver over to the marine band and let my mind go back to the problem at hand as I watched the activities on the cliff. Darkness had fallen, but the working area was as light as day as the huge trucks wound their way in, off the partly constructed Causeway and up to the loading area. The large floodlights on the shovels swung back and forth as they dug into the rock slides that had been blasted from the cliff face to load slabs of stone weighing many tons onto the waiting trucks. At times groups of small lights appeared as workmen in miners' caps appeared from the tunnel that had been dug for the charges that loosened the stone.

I was making this trip against my will but there didn't seem to be anything I could do about it. We hadn't been catching any fish handy to our home port of Canso, but the Prince Edward Island fleet of draggers had been getting good catches fifteen to twenty miles north northeast from Cheticamp off the north coast of Cape Breton. The boats of the Island fleet were bigger and better than ours, but a few boats of our size managed to get good trips so our manager was wondering why we couldn't get one too. I knew it wasn't good judgement to go into North Bay at that time of year in such a small boat. In a few days, navigation would be closed in these waters and even the big steel-beam trawlers would be called out by their owners because their insurance no longer covered them in that part of the ocean. Harbours were miles apart and when the north winds and snow struck, it was dangerous to be out in small boats, especially with a good catch of fish aboard. I had gone over all these arguments in my mind many times in the last few days and even voiced them to my three-man crew, but their silence said, "Other boats are doing it! Why can't we?"

As these thoughts were going through my mind, I could hear the ship-to-ship conversation of the boats fishing about ninety miles away. They were landing fifteen hundred to two thousand pounds of flat fish for an hour-and-a-half tow and I was tempted to throw caution to the winds and head for the fishing ground at full speed. However, as I looked out of the wheel-house window and watched the large snowflakes drift down from the lead dome that formed the sky overhead to disappear in the murky waters of the Strait, the old uneasiness returned and I decided to tie up at Port Hawkesbury for a few hours and get the forecast at midnight.

I felt better as we headed north northwest by the end of the Causeway at about 1:00 A.M. Every time I walked back to the wheel-house through the dark hours of the night, I could see the reflection of the floodlights as the work progressed on the Causeway.

Fishing was fairly good and the crew of three were kept busy between tows putting the fish below in the fish hole and icing them in the pens. I was still uneasy about the weather and by Friday morning we were receiving snow and small craft warnings. At two o'clock we hauled back, stowed our net and doors and started on our way. My idea was to run down the middle of the bay between Cape Breton Island and Prince Edward Island. After everyone had a few hours of sleep, we'd haul in for Henry Island and hope the snow would hold up to get down through the Strait. I hadn't had any sleep since we had left Port Hawkesbury Tuesday midnight outside of a few catnaps caught in the wheel-house. At six o'clock I crawled wearily into Horace's bunk and went to sleep immediately. Two hours and twenty minutes later, I awoke to a terrible bump. I jumped out of the bunk only to be knocked down by another bump. We were ashore. The visibility had been cut down by snow and the first thing we knew, we were in the breakers. Every time the boat went down

in the trough of a sea, we'd hit; then the next sea would pick us up and we'd keep turning. I couldn't see how we were still afloat after all the pounding we'd taken.

Ross had gone straight to the engine room and came back to report we were making water quite fast and he had started the bilge pump. The wind had increased by now to twenty-five miles per hour and at times the snow was quite heavy. About this time, the men on deck stopped pumping. Within five minutes the water level rose considerably. It would take two pumps at full capacity to handle the leaks.

Both pumps plugged up several times and it looked as if we'd have to abandon ship. I told the men I'd set a course for Souris and if they couldn't keep the pumps going, we'd have to take our chances in the dory. Austin brought the flashlight, life belts and batteries from the cabin. Before he got back with these provisions, Ross arrived to report there were six inches of water over the floor. I told him to go down once more and try to get the pump started.

After he left, I told Austin of his new job. I said, "You stand there and pray and don't stop until I tell you, regardless of what happens." He took the handrail on the side of the wheel-house in one hand, his cap in the other, and there he stood and prayed. I've often thought I'd like to have a tape recording of that prayer. I'm sure it must be recorded in heaven be-cause Ross got the pump going again and neither pump stopped again that night.

We were able to raise one of the Can-so draggers on the radio telephone and contacted Canso Marine Radio. At my suggestion, he called the manager of the fish plant in Souris and told him to have his crew there to take our fish out if we should make it in.

When we got near Souris we looked over by the wheel-house to where Aus-tin, cap in hand, eyes closed, was still praying. We made it in, landed our fish and within three days we were back fishing. "All's well that ends well."
—Keith Guptill

*Marine photographer and artist Gilbert van Ryckevorsel took this picture of a blue–fin tuna near the Canso Causeway.*

Gilbert van Ryckevorsel is a marine photog-rapher and artist who has spent a lifetime exploring the underwater worlds of North Atlantic coastal and inland waters. His work has been featured on several Canadian postage stamps and has appeared in most major nature publications, including *National Geographic* and *The Atlantic Salmon*. In the following article, Gilbert shares one of his underwater discoveries near the Causeway.

## "THE UNDERWATER STORY"

The closing of the Canso Channel changed an important passageway for marine life; indeed, it closed off that throughway altogether, and spe-cies involved now have to swim around the northern tip of Cape Breton to ac-cess the Bay of St. Lawrence or the open Atlantic Ocean. One of the most promi-nent oceanic species migrating for eons through that channel is the blue-fin tuna. These fish are top predators in the oceanic pyramid of life. They follow and live off migrating schools of mackerel and herring that swim north in the spring and return south in the fall. Of course, fishermen knew this fact well as their seasonal success depended on these migrations. However, when the Causeway was finished, huge schools of oceanic travellers were blocked off from the routes they knew so well. Schools of mackerel would turn aimlessly in Aulds Cove and the blue-fin tuna predators would show themselves leaping high out of the water around the bay, feasting on their prey and looking out over the water for clues as to where to turn for their traditional passage. From the highway downhill towards the Causeway, the travelling public would view a spectacle of leaping giant fish. On the Causeway itself, close-up observation enabled many travellers to watch this unique phenomenon for as long as it lasted. Aulds Cove fishermen took sport fishermen out on the bay and many had the thrill of a lifetime hooking on to a

five-hundred to thousand-pound giant tuna.

Other species, too, found their passage blocked and slowly new orientations turned ocean migrations to northerly passages. The lobster fishery temporarily benefited from these changes. Sport divers would observe many a large specimen of *Homarus americanus* hiding amongst the rock-filled base of the Canso Causeway. Even these slow-moving marine creatures travelled surprising distances during their spawning season in their never-ending search for better feeding grounds.

One can still see many mackerel and herring trap nets along the Canso Causeway, telling us that indeed it takes generations to change gene-embedded orientation with fish. The spectacular antics of milling mackerel, herring and leaping schools of blue-fin tuna are a result of the Causeway connection between Cape Breton and mainland Nova Scotia.
—Gilbert van Ryckevorsel

Did you know? The blocking of the natural tide has caused a one-degree difference in the temperature of the water. The water on the south side of the Causeway, although only eighty feet away from the water on the north side, is one degree warmer. The tide now rises and falls six inches more than it did before the Strait of Canso was closed. The tide on one side of the Causeway is nearly one metre (three feet) higher than it is on other side.

The completion of the Causeway may have contributed to a number of unforeseen ecological disasters when the natural seaport at Point Tupper became the only accessible deepwater port in the western hemisphere able to accommodate the world's largest oil tankers. Eventually, the unthinkable happened and one of these oil tankers ran into trouble in Chedabucto Bay. On February 4, 1970, the Liberian tanker *Arrow* ran aground on Cerberus Rock and sank, with half its cargo of Bunker 'C' oil seeping into the bay. By February 12, approximately 2.5 million gallons of black oil had escaped to pollute the waters of the bay and the surrounding shoreline.

At the time of the accident, little was known about how best to clean up such a disaster because no major oil spill of Bunker 'C' fuel oil had been experienced in cold water. Also, the problem of removing oil from a submerged tanker had not been encountered to date. Before the task force was able to organize a cleanup, about eight thousand tons of oil had escaped and the shorelines of Richmond County were completely polluted from Point Michaud to Lower River. Cleanup efforts would continue through to the fall of 1970. *The Irving Whale* was brought to the scene to help with the cleanup; this ship later sank, causing its own cleanup concerns near Prince Edward Island.

In a roundabout way, the Causeway may also have contributed to the greatest ship collision of its time. In 1977 a collision involving two voyaging Very Large Crude Carriers (VLCCs), *Venpet* and *Venoil*, occurred twenty-two miles off the coast of Cape Agulhas at the southern tip of Africa on December 16, 1977. The *Venpet* had left Point Tupper after discharging its cargo of Iranian crude. It was bound for Kharg Island, Iran's primary oil export terminal, at the time of the accident.

According to marine historian R. F.

Latimer, it was not until 1997 that the tanker port of Antifer, located twelve miles north of LeHavre, France, was built to handle the huge tonnage that would match the capability Point Tupper already possessed.

Did you know? The current all tackle world angling record for blue-fin tuna, 679.0 kg, was for a fish caught off Aulds Cove in the Strait of Canso, Gulf of St. Lawrence, Nova Scotia, in 1979.

*A time–honoured tradition in high schools across our country is to have individual pictures taken of every graduating student, to give to friends and family members. The 1997 Graduation Committee at SAERC (Strait Area Education and Recreation Centre, in Port Hawkesbury), the nearest high school to the Canso Causeway, chose to have their class grad photo taken in front of the bridge at the canal on the Causeway. According to Rilla McLean, a volunteer researcher and record–keeper for events involving the Causeway, "The members of the SAERC class of 1997 had their class grad picture under the 'Welcome to Cape Breton' sign on the Canso Causeway because it signified another milestone in their lives. For more than seventy percent of the class, their initial milestone had occurred eighteen years earlier as they drove with their mothers over the Causeway and under the welcome sign for the very first time, on their way home to Cape Breton from St. Martha's Hospital in Antigonish on the mainland."*

# CHAPTER 6

# THE CAUSEWAY AND THE CANAL

## THE NEXT FIFTY YEARS

Tourists and those who are not hurrying to get to their destinations often enjoy watching the boats go through the locks at the canal on the eastern side of the Causeway. Nancy Beaton, Director of Rehabilitation of the NSCPA, wrote of a trip she made as a child with her grand-uncle Hubert and aunt Tillie to visit her grandmother, Jane Coady, in Cape Breton. On their way home after the visit a boat was going through the canal. They got out of the car for a closer look. "My uncle made a big deal out of the occasion. He talked to me about the Causeway and the bridge and explained how and why the whole thing was happening. It was the first time I remembered having to stop there and, therefore, the first time I remember being conscious of the whole Causeway crossing and the bridge that opens for water traffic."

On the other hand, regular commuters who are held up at the canal waiting for the swing bridge to move back into position while a boat comes into the lock have been known to ask this question: "Why do they open the swing bridge so early?" To the anxious motorist waiting in a line-up while the bridge is open and the ship is far off, there are times the bridge appears to be opening several minutes ahead of when the lock will be needed. Don Curry, a former canal superintendent, explained that according to an agreement signed when the Causeway and the canal were built, except for cases when an ambulance has phoned ahead to say it is coming through, priority has to be given to ship traffic. When asked why the bridge is opened when the ship is so far away he explained, "The harbour pilots want the bridge open far enough ahead so that they have time to turn the ship if something goes wrong."

During the hot summer months in the late eighties and early nineties, people travelling across the Causeway experienced more than the usual number of delays and often were caught waiting for the swing bridge to move back into place so they could get to work or to an appointment on time.

In the extreme heat during the summer of 1991, the metal on the swing bridge expanded and there were frequently lengthy delays while travellers waited for the bridge to move back to its locked position. Pictures in *The Reporter* showed firemen from the Port Hastings Fire Department hosing down the underside of the bridge in an attempt to cool and contract the expanding metal, thus allowing the boats which had been delayed for up to eight hours to pass into the lock. Although Don Curry allowed that the bridge never stayed open for longer than thirty-five minutes at a time, this was long enough to cause the heavy summer traffic to back up in all directions. By November the provincial government announced it had awarded a contract to replace the steel Bailey bridge and improve the approaches on either side of the bridge.

None of these delays were as lengthy as those before the days of the Causeway. One irate driver sent a letter expressing his frustration to *The Sydney Post* in August of 1925. "Sir: Has it occurred to anyone to comment on transportation facilities across the Strait of Canso? There is no doubt that they have commented but it was probably unfit for print!" The author of the letter went on to suggest if a motorist arrived at Port Hawkesbury six seconds after dusk, he was informed the ferry was tied up for the night. Although treaties ensued, they were of no avail. "The genial

captain of the *Edith C* turns to adamant as the shades of evening fall, and informs you that he has fulfilled his contract and that's that!"

Doug Fritzell of Truro experienced a different type of delay during a scary Causeway crossing back in 1962: "My father, Warren, a CNR worker, decided to take my brother and me on a 'busman's holiday' to visit family members in South Bar near Sydney. Fog and mist over the Causeway led to the driver making a serious mistake in judging the length of time it took him to cross the Causeway and arrive at the swing bridge. When the dayliner neared the bridge it was open, having allowed a ship to pass through the locks only moments before. I remember the train skidding along the ties. Fortunately for all concerned, the dayliner hit the derailing system, a device that safeguards against the train going into the canal when the bridge is open, and the train with its passengers was saved from a serious accident."

It is the job of the person running the controls in the cabin on top of the swing bridge to open the train derailers, pull the stabilizers and track wedges, operate the switches to put on the red lights and lower the security gates, in order to assure safety of rail and road traffic approaching the swing bridge.

Relatives returning to visit their home in Cape Breton have developed interesting traditions to celebrate their arrival at the Causeway. According to Geraldine MacIsaac, her uncle Angus MacDonald, a miller from Glencoe, "was a bachelor who lived in Boston and came home to Cape Breton every summer. He liked a little drink. When he approached New Glasgow, he'd have a wee sip, at Antigonish, another; when he crossed the Causeway, however, he took a much larger sip to welcome himself to Cape Breton!"

While some may take a sip to celebrate their homecoming, others dance for joy. Dancing is so much a part of the island's culture that when Edna MacDonald's twin uncles reached the Causeway on their way home from Ontario, they stopped to express their joy: "One whistled a jig while the other danced and the traffic waited." However, the twins weren't the first to dance on the Causeway. Donald Beaton Riley grew up in Port Hastings and his home was on the current site of the swing bridge at the Canso Causeway. According to local legend, Riley loved to dance anywhere and everywhere. While dancing at the Causeway's opening in August 1955, he suddenly stopped and announced to the people in the grandstand that he was dancing in the same spot where he was born. Riley's bronzed shoes are on display at the Gut of Canso Museum. The dancer's epitaph reads: "Donald Beaton Riley, November 23, 1897– October 19, 1972—Lord of the Dance."

So at the sight of the Causeway, some had a nip and some danced a jig, but perhaps even more counted their money to make sure they had enough to pay tolls for their return trip home. Some Cape Bretoners remembered their first experiences working away from home in the big city (Halifax). They hadn't

been there long when they set a goal to save enough money to make the trip home for the weekend. The much-anticipated day finally arrived and they piled into the car to make the long-awaited trip. With the first glimpse of the Causeway around Harvre Boucher they all gave a whoop of joy. Their next concern sent them digging in their wallets and counting their change, praying they had enough to pay both the toll and the admission to the Friday night dance in Judique.

Not all memories of crossing the Causeway are happy ones. Due to extreme weather conditions, many have had the unfortunate experience of being involved in an accident while trying to cross the Causeway. Other accidents happened on beautiful sunny days, like the time the tarp covering a load on the back of an eighteen-wheeler let go and the flying metal clamp cut through the side of a Volvo and opened a gash in a passing RV like they were sardine tins. There have been reports of Causeway accidents involving as many as twenty-one cars and boats; one, a fishing boat owned by Mike and Kathleen Gerard, fell victim to high winds and crashed into the Causeway December 2, 1997. Sadly there have also been accidents that have claimed lives, like the one in March of 1977 that took the life of Trish Handspiker's mother, Mrs. Rita (Fraser) Forrestall.

In 1955, commuter tickets for crossing the Causeway were valid for one month and frequent travellers were able to save fifty cents over the cost of a one-way crossing, which was seventy-five cents. By September 15, 1980, frequent travellers in passenger vehicles could purchase twenty-five tokens for $5.00, but the infrequent travellers and tourists paid $1.50. However, by 1980, instead of stopping to pay a fare coming to and going from the island, the full fare was paid upon crossing the island.

The first toll booth keepers were men laid off from their jobs on the ferries. Although unpredictable weather no longer posed the same degree of danger to the toll booth keepers as it did when they were crossing the Strait on the ferries, their new job did prove to be challenging at times. One attendant had a heart racing experience when a run-away truck hit the toll booth. The attendant managed to escape by the side door just as the truck hit the other side of the booth, causing the structure to collapse.

Donald Duncan, his wife, Frances, and their children Ian, Gregg and Lynn lived in Port Hawkesbury from 1974 to 1982. Donald had reason to question the government's policy when it came to issuing rebates on toll tickets.

## "CAUSEWAY TOKENS & CHANGE"

I arrived at the job in December of 1973 and lived in an apartment until my family arrived from Toronto in May. Shortly after arriving in Port Hawkesbury, I bought a car and ten tokens for the Causeway for $5.00. I was told the tokens belonged to the car and not to me, meaning that the tokens were not transferable. I went to Fredericton in January to my mother's funeral and on the way home, I ran the car off the road near Havelock, New Brunswick, in a snowstorm and almost killed myself. I wrecked the car and spent three days in the Moncton hospital recovering from cracked ribs. Three weeks later, after convalescing in Toronto with my family and buying another car, my wife and I drove back to Moncton, picked up the contents of the wrecked car from my brother's house and travelled on to Port Hawkesbury.

The tokens that I bought for the car to cross the Causeway cost $5.00 for ten tokens. A single trip across the Causeway cost $1.50. There were seven tokens left in the wrecked car. So I sent the tokens to the office that looks after the Causeway and asked for a refund of $3.50 ($0.50 X 7). I received a reply which said "Total cost of tokens— $5.00, Tokens used—3 @ $1.50 = $4.50." Enclosed was a postal money order to the amount of $0.50. Being a law-abiding citizen who tries to do what's right, I cashed the money order.
—Donald Duncan

The price of the Causeway crossing was part of the negotiated price when two well-known horse-breeders, Donald Rankin from Frenchvale, Cape Breton, and Frank Daniels from Truro, did business. According to Steve Sutherland of "Maritime Noon," Frank and Donald traded horses twenty-five to thirty times a year. Before leaving home, one of the men would call the other and arrange to meet at the Causeway. However, the story has it that on the day of trading it was quite usual to drive past Frank Daniel's truck parked on the Aulds Cove side of the Causeway where it stayed for hours while he had a snooze. If one drove across the Causeway, it was not at all unusual to see Donald Rankin's truck parked on the side of the road where apparently he too was having a sleep. Those who witnessed the proceedings said the "sleep off" would often last for several hours before one or the other of the men would give in and cross the Causeway where the price-haggling would begin in earnest. The cost of the toll was always part of all trading transactions.

The roadway from the mainland to the island was only part of the Causeway construction project in 1955. Near the Cape Breton side are a lock system and canal that allow all but the largest ships to move through the Strait of Canso. The steel swing bridge over the canal carries a prominent sign, "Welcome to Cape Breton" and it is the setting for the following stories.

Before water was allowed into the locks, Victor Kyte was appointed as the first superintendent of the Canso Canal where he served for twenty-three years. Prior to being appointed to this position, Kyte, a veteran, was superintendent of the canal at St. Peters. His daughter, Helen Kyte Darker, tells his story.

## "OVERLOOKING THE CANSO CANAL"

Our home was located in Port Hastings overlooking the canal. During the construction of the Causeway there was a shortage of houses to buy or rent in the area so the government converted an office used by one of the construction engineers during the building of the Causeway to make a home for us. There was a concrete vault in the end of the closet in my bedroom. During construc-

Twenty-five years after the causeway was completed, the tolls amounted to eleven million dollars, less than one half the total cost of the Causeway. Tolls were removed from the Causeway on Friday, December 13, 1991.

tion it had been used to lock up the engineer's drawings and plans. When we were living there, my mother used it to as a place to store her pickles during the winter. That house was the only place I know where it could be windy on all four sides all the same time.

I loved to play on the swing bridge when it was turning and although some of the busy attendants threatened to throw me in the canal for my actions, I knew they wouldn't throw me into the dangerous waters.

In winter, when the phone for the canal office would ring in the house, I would run upstairs to answer it and pretend I was my father's secretary. The ship called through on a land line and I'd still say "over and out." They usually called two days ahead of their arrival. I'd look out the window to see the ice conditions and tell them if they needed to call ahead for an ice-breaker to clear a path before they got to the canal. Drift ice, or *an deigh mhor* as the locals referred to it, could come in as early as November and stay until March or April.

Once a wooden ship used to train Belgian sea cadets ran into the south lock and did considerable damage to the lock. The ship came in under sail, although it did have auxiliary motors aboard. It earned the distinction of being the first ship to damage the canal.

It seemed like every year around

Thanksgiving there would be a severe storm and the family would watch helplessly out our front windows as the boats were battered about. One year *Matheson*, a canal boat named after Kenny Matheson, superintendent of the St. Peter's canal, sank along with several others.

Those who travel across the Causeway on a regular basis are aware of the area's peculiar weather patterns. On a hot summer's day, breezes off the water cause the area to be several degrees cooler than inland and it's not unusual when the wind is bustling up the Strait to lose sight of the roadway when a wave of salt spray encompasses your vehicle. At times one of us would be looking out our front window and the weather on the hill around our home would be as clear as a bell, but a storm would be blowing over the Causeway. They called these squalls "Causeway storms." Often the storms were so severe the shift workers travelling from the mill wouldn't be able to get home. They were stranded.

One unique thing I discovered about crossing over the canal bridge was the archway at the Cape Breton side was lower than the bridge opening on the other. Years ago when Port Hawkesbury was experiencing a building boom, builders were bringing prefab houses from the mainland to erect in what is now Tamarac Heights. Much to the embarrassment of the truck driver, the roof of the house he was hauling hit the archway on the Cape Breton side and he couldn't dislodge it from its position, thus blocking traffic in both directions. In the end, he solved the problem by letting the air out of the truck's tires and pulling the flat-bed through the gap.

Our family's special memory of the Causeway happened when we were travelling home from the mainland late at night. After we rounded the corner at Havre Boucher where the lights of the Causeway are first visible, my younger brother said, "Oh look at the Causeway's birthday cake."
—Helen Kyte Darker

## "A DOG'S TALE"

Jeff, our family's dog, enjoyed his seventeen-year stay at our home overlooking the Canso Canal and his well-earned honorary title of Assistant Canal Superintendent. He had the run of the canal. Jeff's favourite time of year was summer. His gait quickened whenever he heard the sound of bagpipes at the tourist bureau that overlooks the Causeway. Somehow he never forgot that tourists had food, and Jeff was particularly adept at begging. Other successful begging episodes occurred whenever the canal staff took their coffee break. Part German shepherd and part cocker spaniel,

Jeff made sure he was sitting in the canal attendant's line of vision where he was best able to send a message of guilt if the attendant failed to give a poor starved dog with long floppy ears a tasty morsel. Jeff's keen ears also told him when the bridge was swinging to let a ship pass through the locks. At the first sound of the warning bell he would hightail it down to the roadway where the cars were lined up in front of the barricade. Once there, he proceeded to move from one car to another, begging for food.

Jeff's most successful episode was the time he hobbled beside his master, Victor Kyte, canal superintendent, to the lock to greet *Texaco Chief*. The cook lost his heart to the poor dog hobbling beside the canal with a cast on its hind leg and as a result, he demonstrated his affection by making a trip to the galley. Soon he returned with a gift any dog would appreciate: a leg of lamb. Thereafter, Jeff would stand watch and, recognizing the ship before it was any larger than a dot out on the horizon, he'd hightail it to the lock and wait patiently for the cook's new contribution to his diet.
—Helen Kyte Darker & Michael Kyte

After 1955, Point Tupper did lose its railway terminal and the little community was forced to change from a residential area to an industrial one. The ice-free port made it possible for ships to use this terminal all year round. However, an extra advantage for those using the Strait to ship goods to market was that for nearly eight months of the year, ships could go through the lock, thus taking a shortcut on their way to the St. Lawrence. During the sixties this route was frequently used by oil tankers carrying their loads of crude to the refinery that once was located there.

In 1963, Gary Moore was a young man, sailing on the *Texaco Warrior*, an oil tanker and sister ship to *Texaco Chief* that frequently passed through the short canal separating the Atlantic Ocean from the Northumberland Strait when the Canso Causeway was built. His story is a tribute to his late mother, Christie Moore, who illustrated that a mother's love for her son will surpass any obstacle—by land or by sea.

## "COOKIES AT THE CANAL"

One particular memory will always be a part of who I am today, for it helped me realize the never-ending love, commitment, and sacrifices parents will make for their children throughout their lives.

I was nineteen years of age, a very exciting time for a boy who had grown up in Pleasant Bay, a tiny fishing village of several hundred people located at the tip of Cape Breton Island. Whenever I knew that we would be passing through the canal, I would contact Mom. She would be so excited about my occasional visits that she would travel more than a hundred miles to see me. Time and weather were irrelevant to her. Day or night, snow, rain, or fog, she would always be there to greet me with freshly baked butterscotch pies, cookies or other sweet treats which, today, are still favourite recipes among my own children and grandchildren. She would give me these few comforts of home as I continued on my journey, always homesick for the Highlands of Cape Breton. Our time together was brief, only fifteen or twenty minutes, just long enough for the captain to complete his paperwork. Then off we would go, on to the Great Lakes, but my lonely heart was always replenished and my strength restored by the sweet gestures of my mother.

Those memories of my passages through the canal, made possible only because of the Canso Causeway, are probably among the most fondly recalled of my life. Today, as I make trips back and forth across the Causeway and into the Highlands to visit my brother Kenneth who still lives at our childhood home in Pleasant Bay, I always recall those voyages that forever forged a love that knew no boundaries between a mother and her son.

—Gary Moore

Just as Gary Moore's mother drove miles to demonstrate her love with her care packages, Rachel MacFarlane's grandfather, Bob MacPherson, walked miles to provide care and to demonstrate his love for his family. It was said that Bob actually walked through snow so deep that he found himself on the roofs of cars, using their aerials as his guide.

## "WALKING TO WORK"

*Bob MacPherson on his last day of work.*

My grandfather, Robert Mansfield MacPherson, began working at the Causeway when it opened in 1955. His job was to operate the swing bridge for boats crossing the Strait of Canso. He lived in the community of Havre Boucher with his wife, Mary Helen, and his family of nineteen children.

In his twenty-two years at the Canso Causeway, he never missed a day of work. He always worked the 4:00 P.M. to midnight shift, often walking to and from work, some fifteen kilometres. In recent years, other family members and I have encountered stories from community members who offered him a drive when they met him along the way. One thing they always said was that he would never get into a car until he knew you were from the area.

Truman, one of his ten sons, lived in Mulgrave and worked at the heavy water plant on the Cape Breton side of the Causeway. Like his father, he worked the

4:00 P.M. to midnight shift. The pair would often meet and walk together on their way home. Truman recalls the winter of 1969–70 as an especially cold and blustery one. They would have to walk on the opposite side of the bay, otherwise ocean waves would soak them from head to toe. Their clothes would be frozen stiff by the time they got to the end of the Causeway, making the walk home a long one.

My aunts and uncles have shared many stories of their father with us, his grandchildren. One of my favourites is about how Grampie used to save all the newspapers and magazines that he could get his hands on. You see, he often sent mail to friends and family living away. He would use the papers to wrap the packages tightly to ensure a safe delivery to their destination. The leftover papers were carefully wrapped in twine, which he would take to work with him. From his station above the Causeway, he would drop the newspapers onto the decks of ships as they passed through the locks. His purpose in doing this was to provide some reading material for the crew. Many of the men on the passing boats spent many long weeks and months on the ocean and he thought that they would enjoy catching up on the news of the day.

Another story that was passed on to me was about a pair of binoculars that were left on the Causeway. It was some time during the 1960s when my grandfather came across the glasses on his way home from work. Inside the case he found a couple's name and the area they were visiting from. Aside from their name and address, a hundred dollar bill was tucked inside. After some time and a lot of searching, he found the couple's address in the States and returned the binoculars, money and all. I especially liked this story as it showed his character, one of honesty and determination.
—Rachel MacFarlane

A would-be writer wanted to write a fictional story about the destruction of the Causeway. She imagined such an act being necessary in order "to prevent an invasion of the island," and she wanted to know who she should get in touch with for details on the best way to de-stroy the Causeway. If the storms in the Strait area are anything to go by, then the surest way to destroy the Causeway would be from a storm sent by Mother Nature herself.

On January 11, 1994, a hurricane-scale wind, clocked at 90 mph at the Canal, severely damaged the Aulds Cove waterfront. Heavy seas battered the Causeway, leaving boulders, driftwood and dead fish strewn across it. The cleanup committee's tools included dump trucks and front-end loaders.

Doug Myra recalled a time he was travelling to Sydney with his parents. As they approached the Causeway a sudden storm created poor road conditions and visibility: "My mother said we shouldn't go across but my father said, 'No, we should go.' We started out but we couldn't see anything. My father stopped by the side of the road and said, 'We can't go further until a plough comes by.' Soon we saw flashing lights. An RCMP car pulled in behind us to advise us on conditions and visibility. The next thing we saw were the lights of a snowplough, but he didn't see us. Instead he ploughed into the RCMP cruiser, ramming it into the back of our car. Our family never did cross the Causeway that day. We were taken by ambulance to the hospital in Truro."

Master Seamen Peter Lewis was born in North Sydney and moved to Port Hood when he was still very young. He remembers a day when his parents stopped at the Causeway to watch a large container ship go through the locks. The event left a lasting impression.

## "THE DIFFERENCE A WAVE MAKES"

We went over to see this wonderful sight and wave to the people on board. To my surprise we received no response from the workers. As a youngster I really could not understand why no one waved back and I carried a bad memory for a long time.

I am presently serving in my twenty-third year as member of the Canadian navy. In the summer of 1982 I found out that our ship was going to go through the locks at the Causeway. I was a young ordinary seaman at the time and got very excited that this Cape Bretoner was going to sail through the Canso Causeway. But as we were approaching the locks, the memory of my childhood experience came back. Looking ahead I could see people gathering at the locks to watch the ship approach. It was at this time that I decided that these people would not have the same experience as I did. We waved and talked to all who could hear and see us. I recognized some of the locals and shared some laughs and pictures. This was a special day.

When my wife and I returned to Judique and Port Hood for a visit later that summer, a lot of the kids came over to the house to show me the pictures. The look in their eyes and smiles on their faces erased all my bad memories and made me proud of what I did. Since then, whenever I pull into any port, all people who stop to wave and watch are going to receive the same warm greeting.
—Peter Lewis

## "SWINGING FROM A SWING BRIDGE IN A STORM"

I am the first female bridge-tender to work on the Canso Causeway swing bridge and I enjoy my work, even though I have worked through some tremendous storms. I have worked this job since May of 1995 but I won't soon forget the night I worked the evening shift in the fall of 2001. Blaise MacNeil, who was working the day shift that day, called me at home to tell me the wind had blown over an empty tractor-trailer on the Causeway and I might have a bit of trouble getting to work because of the traffic tie-up. The call was my first hint that the evening shift wasn't going to be "as usual."

When I got to work, the weather was already miserable. The wind was blowing fiercely and waves were washing over the highway. The tractor-trailer was lying on the westward lane of the highway, about ten car lengths from the west side of the bridge. Traffic was moving slowly in the eastward lane. As often happens in the Strait area, the wind was blowing the rain sideways.

The violent wave action had thrown debris onto the highway, making it dangerous for vehicles to cross the causeway. By early evening, the traffic had to be escorted across by a snow-removal truck. Going ahead of the traffic, the truck cleared the highway of rocks and driftwood. Meanwhile, traffic was building up on both sides of the Causeway.

I was watching this from my vantage point on the bridge. When marine traffic is slow, I bring a book along to help pass the time, but that night the bridge was shaking so hard, my book was moving up and down in front of my face.

As I watched from the westward-facing window, a large picture window I use to see out when I'm swinging the bridge, I noticed it was moving with the wind. I was terrified! I had no idea what I would do if the window were to blow in.

The waves washed out part of the highway on the west side of the Causeway and it became too dangerous to allow people to go across. The traffic finally stopped moving about nine o'clock that night. When I went home the next morning the storm had abated somewhat, but rain and wind still tugged at the bridge. It was nice to get back onto solid ground. I love my work on the bridge but this was one storm I wouldn't want to work through again.
—Annemary Butcher

# CHAPTER 7

# 25 YEARS OF MEMORABLE CROSSINGS

When Yvonne Fox, a volunteer member of the Port Hastings Historical Society, realized that the twenty-fifth anniversary of the Canso Causeway was approaching, she hastily called a public meeting for March 10, 1980, to plan an event to mark the occasion. The group decided on a program that would include the re-enactment of the original opening ceremonies; they invited various government departments and construction personnel involved with the original project to participate. They saw the twenty-fifth anniversary as an excellent time to have a reunion for the men who worked on the project.

On the committee were representatives from several communities from the Strait area. As a result of the meeting, the following people accepted positions to help with the planning: Blair Brewer, chair; Martha MacNeil, co-chair; Brenda Roach, secretary; Kathy MacIsaac, treasurer. Other committee members included Dan MacDonald, Yvonne Fox, Ed MacDonald, Jim Cotter, Beckey MacInnis, Angus Macachern, Rilla McLean, Neil Marple, Lauchie MacDougall, Ian H. MacKinnon, Martin MacKinnon, Mary Campbell Jamieson, Anne MacLean Hughes, Graeme Gagnon, Morag Graham, George Ingraham, Zena Sorge, Gord Isenor, Mary Gillis, Hazen Holmes, Chris Weeks, Jerry MacFarlane, Don Heighton.

Platform guests for these celebrations were: John Buchanan, Premier of Nova Scotia; Hon. Allen J. MacEachen, Deputy Prime Minister of Canada, MP Highlands-Canso; Hon. Justice Angus L. Macdonald Jr. and his wife, Evelyn; Senator Henry Hicks and Mrs. Hicks; Bishop William E. Power of the Antigonish Diocese; Rev. W. S. Smith, Archdeacon of Cape Breton; and Mr. D. W. Blair, Regional Vice-President of Canadian National Railway. Danny Graham sang the National Anthem. One unexpected and uninvited guest also

*The twenty–fifth anniversary of the Causeway's opening. L–R: Premier John Buchanan; Deputy Prime Minister Allen J. MacEachen; and former Premier Henry Hicks.*

*Re–enactment of the opening ceremonies at the twenty–fifth anniversary.*

joined those on the platform: Port Hawkesbury's long-serving mayor, Billy Joe MacLean.

In 1977 Terry Fox, a young man from Port Coquitlam, BC, lost part of his right leg to cancer. Three years later he began a run across Canada to raise money for cancer research. Support for his Marathon of Hope didn't come immediately, but Yvonne Fox (no relation), from Port Hastings, was touched by Terry's heroic journey. For years Yvonne has collected items of interest for the local museum and to her mind Terry's story and his historic crossing of the Causeway was a memory to be preserved for future generations.

## "CROSSING FOR A CAUSE~THE MARATHON OF HOPE CROSSES THE CAUSEWAY"

Twenty-five years after it was constructed, the link between Cape Breton Island and mainland Nova Scotia—the Canso Causeway—took on a special significance at 6:30 in the morning on Sunday May 11, 1980. That was the morning Terry Fox of Port Coquitlam, British Columbia, continued his Marathon of Hope and became the first person to cross the Canso Causeway for a cause. Many would follow.

The previous day, an article in the Saturday Cape Breton Post stated that young Fox from British Columbia had arrived on the ferry at North Sydney. He had started his Marathon of Hope on April 12 in St. John's, Newfoundland, to raise money for cancer research. He planned to run 5,300 kilometres across the country over the next seven months. My mind immediately began to think of some kind of send-off to organize for him as he was leaving Cape Breton Island and crossing the Canso Causeway. I started making telephone calls, the first to the local cancer society volunteers to see what they might be doing. I was reminded by them that cancer month had been in April. I still thought this would be an ideal opportunity to collect donations from people who were missed during the residential canvass. I also suggested that having a one-legged fellow trying to raise money for their cause

*Terry Fox with Yvonne Fox*

• 85 •

*Mayor Billy Joe MacLean of Port Hawkesbury,*
*Terry Fox, and George Fox of Port Hastings.*

who owned the local Ford dealership, would be taking Terry and his friend Doug Alward to supper and we were invited.

After supper, I continued to make telephone calls trying to get a crowd assembled for early Sunday morning. I made a "Good Luck Terry" sign to hang on a post. I had it announced at the dance in the fire hall that Terry would be going back out on the Trans-Canada Highway and picking up where he left off on Saturday. He would be running down to the Port Hastings rotary around 6:00 A.M. I called and left a message with Mayor Billy Joe MacLean of Port Hawkesbury.

The following morning when Terry came jogging down the highway, there were only a handful of us there to greet him. We listened to his frustration about the Nova Scotia Cancer Society not making better use of him. He was prepared to speak to groups and organizations, but nothing was arranged by local or provincial cancer societies. George Fox, the chief of the Port Hastings Fire Department, presented him with a check, and Mayor MacLean of Port Hawkesbury was there to wish him bon voyage and make a commitment of a donation from the town of Port Hawkesbury.

was a unique opportunity for them. Of course, the fact that he would be leaving the island via the Canso Causeway, the ribbon of highway through the ocean, was a motivation as well.

By this time, I was wondering just where he was on his journey along the Trans-Canada Highway between North Sydney and Port Hastings. I made a couple of calls to people in Whycocomagh and Glendale to see if he had been spotted. I then sent my husband out to check. When he returned, I found that our friends Bob and Linda MacKeigan,

I gave Terry nine self-addressed, stamped postcards to be sent back to me as he travelled through the provinces. I also gave him a small poster with a poem entitled "It Couldn't Be Done" by Edgar Albert Guest, which I'm told Terry kept on the wall of the van and apparently read every night. One verse of the poem reads:

*There are thousands to tell you it cannot be done*
*There are thousands to prophesy failure*
*There are thousands to point out to you one*
*by one*
*The dangers that wait to assail you*
*But just buckle in with a bit of a grin,*
*Just take off your coat and go to it.*
*Just start in to sing and tackle the thing*
*That "cannot be done" and you'll do it.*

Pictures were taken against the backdrop of the Causeway, then across the Canso Causeway they went—Doug in the van and Terry following with his peculiar gait. Meeting those two young men from British Columbia made a lasting impression on me. I admired Terry's vibrant personality, which gave him the energy, enthusiasm and vision to want to do the marathon. I also recognized Doug's quiet dedication to all of the behind-the-scenes work, and his patience in waiting for Terry to catch up to him as they travelled down the road.

Later, when Terry had been forced to quit and all the country rallied to raise money, I wished that an important lesson had been learned by Canadians everywhere, a lesson that would leave a legacy beyond Terry and his Marathon of Hope: that everyone has a unique personality and strengths to contribute to the betterment of a project, the community and the country. If Doug Alward had said "no way" to Terry's idea in the first place, Terry wouldn't have been able to run a single kilometre. Don't forget Terry, but whenever someone asks for help on a new idea or project, instead of shooting it down with protests of "it can't be done" or "it's never been done," be a Doug: step up and do what you can.
—Yvonne Fox

*Tourism Accessibility Committee organized a breakfast at Smitty's on April 16, 1997, for the Dave Shannon Cross Canada Tour. L–R: back row, Bob Fougere, Ed MacDonald, Sheila Hearn, Muriel Gionet MacNeill, Ellen Cecchetto; front row, Adam Cooke, Rilla McLean, Dave Shannon*

When the Trans Canada Trail Relay crossed the Causeway in 2000, Rilla McLean of Port Hawkesbury was the first wheelchair participant to carry the official water bottle for the team.

Rick Hansen and well wishers at the Causeway. A paraplegic at the age of 15, Rick travelled 40,000 km starting in 1985 and raised 26 million dollars in support of people with spinal cord injuries.

Stephanie McClellan and the On Wings Like Eagles tour after they crossed the Causeway. L–R: Holding the sign, Carmen Palmer and Sharon Young; below, Joel Corapi, Michael Hey, Ben Anible, Stephanie McClellan

Several times since Terry Fox's groundbreaking run across it in 1980 the Causeway has been used as a stage to bring attention to a particular issue or cause. Rilla McLean, a member of the Strait Accessibility Awareness Committee, writes of fourteen small wheels, two wheelchairs and two handcycles crossing the Causeway.

## "SMALL WHEELS ACROSS THE CAUSEWAY"

They journeyed not by two feet but by three or four small wheels: Rick Hanson, Dave Shannon, John Ryan and Stephanie McClellan all crossed the Causeway and the country for a cause they strongly believed in. I met them at the Causeway and was inspired by their abilities.

The first one occurred in September 12, 1986. A young man was completing his journey around the world and travelling home to British Columbia across Canada by manual wheelchair. By the time he reached the Canso Causeway, Rick Hansen had already pushed his wheelchair more than 18,357 miles through thirty-four countries. He signed autographs and posed for pictures with the children while appearing to have all the time in the world. Through his Man in Motion World Tour this paraplegic raised awareness of the abilities of people in wheelchairs and the problems they

confront and solve each day.

My next "small wheels" encounter came on April 16, 1997. Because this was the second involving a person in a wheelchair travelling across Canada, it did not have the support or publicity of the first. However, there was a major difference. Dave Shannon became the first quadriplegic to travel across the country in a power wheelchair. My most memorable moment of his visit came as we waited by the bridge at the Causeway. We had called for an RCMP escort for Dave because of the strong gusts and frequent waves breaking on the rocks, sending cascades of water over the road. Dave, dressed in his thermal suit and giant-sized mittens and boots, couldn't wait to tackle the Causeway. My last glimpse of this articulate and inspiring actor/lawyer/cross-country traveller was of a small shape at the far end of the Causeway moving steadily westward behind the flashing light of a police cruiser. In early October, I received a call and the voice said, "Hi, it's Dave. We've arrived in Vancouver." His odyssey was complete. His message that disabled people can overcome phenomenal barriers reached thousands of Canadians.

Two years later, in 1999, I had my third "small wheels" encounter at the Causeway. John Ryan, a paraplegic realtor from Whistler, British Columbia, had a twenty-one-speed, three-wheel-cycle operated by hand pedals. His Regeneration Tour hoped to raise five million dollars for research into spinal cord regeneration. On May 17 on a hill overlooking the Causeway, a red-nosed, hoarse-voiced middle-aged woman having a bad hair day and sitting in a wheelchair was the only person other than Steve the driver to greet John Ryan. Not even the media came as arranged.

In 1999, Stephanie McClellan cycled from Vancouver to Ottawa. Then in 2001, she mounted her three-wheeled, hand-propelled cycle in Ottawa and headed east to finish a cross-Canada trek. On August 7, Stephanie arrived at the Causeway much earlier than expected so I told her to wait there un-til the welcoming committee arrived. Fortunately while the six members of the On Wings Like Eagles tour waited, they were entertained by a playful whale in the waters on the north side of the Causeway. When they finally did cross the Canso Causeway going east, a freight train from the Cape Breton and Central Nova Railway was crossing the Causeway coming west. Stephanie had wavers on both sides, happy honkers on her left and a whistle blower on her right.

In the town of Port Hawkesbury, Stephanie continued to deliver her message that people with disabilities are not just people in need, but people who can contribute and serve their communities in meaningful ways. Despite debilitating rheumatoid arthritis and fibromyalgia, Stephanie McClellan completed her cross-Canada tour on schedule at Cape Spear, Newfoundland, at the end of August. She returned to British Columbia, completed her master's degree in theology, and crossed the Causeway again two years later on her way to Gander, Newfoundland, to serve as a United Church minister.
—Rilla McLean

*Garth Haverstock (centre) awaits his turn to carry the Olympic Torch at the Canso Causeway with his grandmother, Frances Dennis (left), and his mother, Carol Haverstock.*

In 1987, as a leadup to the XV Olympic Winter games (February 1988), the Olympic Torch left Athens and travelled by aeroplane to St. John's, Newfoundland. There the official Olympic Torch Run began. Over the next three months runners carried its flame—bound for Calgary—through various Canadian communities, and it crossed the Causeway in Cape Breton on November 20 1987.

Garth Haverstock, from Port Hawkesbury, who used a wheelchair, was proud to help carry the torch across the Causeway.

From her office in Port Hawkesbury, Carol Haverstock, Garth's mother, tells the story of what it meant for her son to carry the torch.

## "THE OLYMPIC TORCH CROSSES THE CAUSEWAY, NOVEMBER 20, 1987."

There are some people who, although they may only be there a short time, leave such an impact they touch your life forever. Such was the case for all those who knew my son, Garth Haverstock. At six, Garth was diagnosed with muscular dystrophy and a few years after this, was confined to a wheelchair. However, in the twelve years he had left after his diagnosis, Garth lived his life with gusto. By the time he was twelve, he had been made an honorary member of the Strait Pirates' Hockey Club, Honorary Junior Fire Chief and campaign assistant for the Nova Scotia fund-drive for muscular dystrophy. Garth was keenly interested in sports and in becoming a fireman. But more important than these titles was the gift Garth gave to others:

*Cyril Gillis running across the Causeway's swing bridge, carrying one of the Olympic Torches used during the official run across Canada.*

*Arnold MacLean and his daughter, Lynn, also carried the Olympic Torch across the Causeway.*

his smile. On the blustery day the Olympic torch crossed the Causeway, a smiling Garth was handed the torch by Cyril Gillis and passed it to Arnold MacLean. —Carol Haverstock

Rilla McLean, a member of the Port Hastings Historical Society, recalls receiving her grandmother Izetta's old hardcover green stamp album as a little girl in the mid-fifties. Nearly a half a century later, this gift led her to apply to Canada Post for a commemorative stamp

of the Canso Causeway, and in the fall of 2004 Canada Post announced that they will bring out a 50-cent domestic stamp picturing the Causeway Bridge as part of its bridge theme in the spring of 2005. Their idea is to picture the open bridge allowing a ship to go through the canal. There will be three other postage stamps in the bridge-theme series. They are: the Angus L. Macdonald Bridge in Halifax, which will also celebrate its fiftieth anniversary this year; the Jacques Cartier Bridge in Montreal, and the Souris Swinging Bridge in Manitoba.

## "A STAMP FOR THE CAUSEWAY?"

When my husband, Jim, and I moved to Cape Breton in 1974, we joined the Sydney Stamp Club. Archie Long, a member of that group and a Sydney postmaster, gave me a very special cover with a machine slogan cancel on the front and the back. It was postmarked "Sydney N.S. 10 AM August 13, 1955." The cancel read "Canso Causeway, Road to the Isle, Opening Ceremony August 13, 1955." (A cancel is a mark the post office puts over the stamp to cancel it so that the stamp can't be used again.)

*Cancellation stamp used for the twenty-fifth anniversary at the Port Hastings Post Office.*

In 1976 we moved to Port Hawkesbury and lived about six kilometres from the Causeway. Three years later, on behalf of the Port Hastings Historical Society, I wrote to the director of the Nova Scotia Postal District to request a special cancellation at the Port Hastings post office for the twenty-fifth anniversary of the Canso Causeway in 1980. On October 15, we received a positive reply that a special hand cancel with a twenty-five-character cancellation message could be used for two months. July and August were chosen. By the third week in June 1980, the steel hammer with the special cancel had not yet arrived from Ottawa. In a panic I contacted Halifax. They produced a rubber stamp cancel that was used by the postmaster Grace Pilgrim on July 2 and 3 until the other cancel arrived. Those two dates of the special cancel that read "Canso Causeway 1955–1980 Port Hastings NS/NE" are collector's items because they were larger than the cancel used from July 4 to August 31.

The Port Hastings Historical Society had special Canso Causeway covers printed for the twenty-fifth anniversary. With information about the cancel in only three newspapers, the society filled orders for three hundred covers but regretfully could not fill all the orders. Requests came from Nova Scotia, other provinces, the United States, England and Holland.

By the year 2000, Canada Post was losing business to electronic mail and courier services and they welcomed requests from post offices across the country to have special pictorial hand cancels.

The efforts of Mindy Haight, a native of Mulgrave and employee of Canada Post in Port Hawkesbury, resulted in the post offices of Port Hastings, Port Hawkesbury and Mulgrave using their pictorial cancels for the first time on January 27, 2003. Alex Boudreau of Port Hawkesbury designed the cancels. All three designs depict the Causeway; Port Hawkesbury and Mulgrave have the same design and the cancel reads "Strait of Canso," whereas Port Hastings has a slightly different design and its cancel reads "Gateway to Cape Breton."

In January 2002 I began my quest for a stamp of the Canso Causeway. A year later, our three-person stamp committee sent a twenty-four page document to the Stamp Advisory Committee requesting a commemorative stamp of the Causeway. The Canso Causeway has been honoured with three different cancels by Canada Post. Now we are waiting expectantly for a stamp to be launched April 1, 2005.
—Rilla McLean

*Pictorial cancels used by the post offices of Port Hastings, Port Hawkesbury and Mulgrave beginning in 2003.*

Throughout history, glimpses of people's lives have been passed on to the next generation through their stories, poems and music. The islanders were great story tellers and used their abilities in their stories and songs to tell about their crossings on the ferries and their longing for a bridge, as in "The Bochan Bridge," by Dan Lewis Macdonald. Since construction began on the Causeway, it too has been a common theme in poems and songs.

## "POETRY AND MUSIC"

The Canso Causeway has the symbolic importance of both "homecoming" and "leaving" to Cape Bretoners. The strong feelings associated with these two events are often expressed in the prose, poetry and music of the island. The Causeway is mentioned in books such as Alistair MacLeod's *No Great Mischief* and heard in songs such as Kenzie MacNeil's "The Island." The fiddle music of Buddy and Natalie Mac-Master and the voices of the Rankins and the Barra MacNeils have crossed the Causeway to entertain people in many countries.

Charlie MacKinnon's "Causeway to the Isle" is a wonderful tribute to its history, culminating in the pipers marching across the Causeway at the official opening. "The Causeway Crossing" (words by Albert MacDonald and music by John Gillis) certainly fits the "leaving but longing to stay" category as does the song "Cape Breton's Crying" (Russell Deveaux; Calum MacPhee; Glen, Brad and Keith MacNeil). The latter song was inspired by a phrase coined by Darrell Jones as he and his friends were leaving Cape Breton to return to work in Ontario. Looking back, they saw the mist suspended over the Causeway. Arnold Sampson's song "Home Again" contains a more upbeat refrain: "Over the Causeway, up to the Margaree...I'm home again. I'll never leave this island anymore." "Causeway Song" was composed by Charlotte Rankin MacInnis of Creignish after the Causeway was completed. It was sung at a Scottish concert in the Stella Maris Parish Hall shortly after the Causeway opened in 1955. The four lines of the chorus were written and sung in Gaelic.

On July 13, 1977, the play The Mulgrave Road Show was first performed at the St. Lawrence Parish Hall in Mulgrave. In this production, two of the songs written by Robert O'Neil, Michael Fahey, Wendell Smith and Gay Hauser are about the road across the water: "My Pile of Rocks" and "The Causeway Song." The latter expresses the negative impact of the Causeway on the town of Mulgrave. That group of four composers birthed the Mulgrave Road Theatre Company, now a professional touring company based in the town of Guysborough.

In 1989, the town of Port Hawkesbury celebrated its centennial. One of the many special activities that year was the formation of the Under the Map theatre group that performed plays depicting the town's history on four consecutive nights using Granville Street as the setting. "Here Comes the Causeway," written by Helen MacDonald and Hilary Fraser with help from members of the community, was sung on the third night in the play *Crossing the Strait*.

In addition to Causeway songs written for piano and guitar, the fiddle and the bagpipe have their own tunes. Queensville resident Dan Hugh MacEachern's fiddle tune "Canso Crossing Hornpipe" was among the tunes published in his first book. A later book included the march "Road to the Isle of New Scotland." Pipe Major Sandy Boyd also composed a tune for the bagpipes entitled "Crossing the Causeway."

The bagpipe, fiddle, guitar, piano and voice have all made their contribution to enshrining the Canso Causeway in music that will live on for generations.
—Rilla McLean

Ever since it was built, people have lined up at the Causeway to watch the ships pass through the canal. From the Royal Yacht Britannia in 1967 to cruise ships, from lobster boats to oil tankers, all have drawn attention from the public and so it was when the tall ships passed through the canal in 1984.

## "A TALL SHIP AT THE CANSO CANAL"

In June 1984 the tall ships sailed through the Canso Canal for the first time. To mark the occasion, the Port Hastings Historical Society decided to honour the first non-North American ship to arrive at the canal. After spending five days in Halifax, the ships were sailing on to Quebec City to celebrate the 450th anniversary of Jacques Cartier's first voyage to North America. There were a few obstacles in our path, but that did not deter us. First, the canal was undergoing major repairs and the opening date was only a week prior to the arrival of the tall ships—if the work went according to schedule. Second, we needed an interpreter, as many of the sailors did not speak English. And we had no idea at what time the non-North American tall ship would arrive. Two problems were quickly resolved.

The workers at the canal completed their job on schedule, and in the Strait area, we were fortunate to have people who spoke French, German, Italian, Polish, Russian, Spanish, and Swedish. All agreed to act as our interpreters. However, we would not know until the day of arrival what language was needed. It was not a problem for most of our bilingual friends—except one. The Polish translator, Dr. Waddeck Guzdziol, could not leave his office and his patients to be at the canal waiting for a tall ship.

Members of the society also contacted some bagpipers and highland dancers to welcome the ships and entertain at the reception. We received excellent cooperation from canal superintendent Don Currie and Coast Guard traffic control centre staff at Eddy Point who had the ships on radar and would be in radio contact with them.

*Tall Ship Gedania, of Poland, at the Causeway.*

Thursday June 14 finally arrived and the Coast Guard called to inform us the first tall ships would arrive in the early afternoon. We contacted the translators and entertainers about the expected arrival time. Two ships from the Netherlands, two from Poland and one from the United Kingdom were leading the flotilla of forty-nine tall ships. Which one would arrive first was still a mystery.

At 2:00 P.M. the canal informed us of a further delay: the ships had slowed down. *Urania* from the Netherlands and *Gedania* from Poland were leading and would arrive by late afternoon. By three o'clock it was evident that *Gedania* would be the first non-North American vessel to arrive at the canal. We called the doctor and told him when to come. We also informed the local radio stations, CIGO and CJFX, of the estimated time of arrival of the ships. Carloads of people came to wave and welcome. Now there were more problems. Our publicity campaign had worked too well. Dr. Guzdziol didn't arrive on time because of the traffic jam. At 4:35 P.M., *Gedania* finally docked at the canal to a typical Cape Breton bagpipe welcome. We could only wonder what was going on in the minds of the unprepared Polish crew as they approached and saw a kilted piper leading a small crowd out to meet them. After only a few moments of uncertainty, the reception warmed up and the

crew enjoyed Cape Breton tea and oatcakes. Dr. Guzdziol translated during the official ceremony, conducted by Inverness County councillor Ed MacDonald. On behalf of the historical society, I presented a Cape Breton plaque to Captain Mieczyslaw Czarniawski and the crew. Mulgrave mayor Allison England presented the captain with a framed aerial photograph of Mulgrave. Representing Port Hawkesbury, Councillor Eric Winsor gave the guests pins engraved with the town crest. Captain Czarniawski, pleased and honoured by the unexpected welcome, made a few presentations on behalf of his vessel. To the historical society, he presented a large brass plaque embossed with the crests of the ship and of the Gdansk Shipyard Yacht Club. He gave me a pennant with the crest of *Gedania* on one side and the crest of the Gdansk Shipyard on the other.

Adding colour to the reception were highland dancers Juanita and Ann MacIntyre, Patti Ann MacLeod, Kim Morgan and Lynn MacDonnell and pipers Ian McKinnon and Cathy Urquhart. Pipers Roddie White and Peter MacMullin also helped pipe some of the other tall ships through the canal. The *Gedania* crew enjoyed this taste of our culture and they took many pictures with the tartan-clad dancers and pipers. After the formalities were finished, the crew returned the hospitality and invited us to visit their vessel. Once aboard, the visitors enjoyed a tour of the vessel and exchanged toasts in Polish, English and Gaelic with a liquid stronger than Cape Breton tea.

The captain asked Dr. Guzdziol to tell us about the strike at the Gdansk Shipyard and the solidarity movement in communist Poland. When the doctor replied that we already knew because it had been in our papers, the captain was surprised. Dr. Guzdziol also said the opportunity to sail on the *Gedania* was considered a great privilege by the crew members.

The Polish government ordered the ship to bypass St. John's, Newfoundland, because Pope John Paul II was visiting there. The captain defied the orders and docked his vessel in the harbour, where the Polish pope blessed it. One of the sailors spoke for all when he said, "We'll be going home a happy crew." —Rilla McLean

One fine June morning in 1984, former Port Hawkesbury residet Marilyn MacPhee noted what appeared to be a two-mast, square-rigged sailing ship sitting in the Strait at the government wharf at the bottom of MacSween Street, where she lived. This was the start of what turned into an unusual day.

*Tall Ship Inca sailing into the Northumberland Strait after coming through the canal.*

## "THE *INCA*"

I drove down to the wharf and greeted the captain and crew of *Inca*. The captain invited me on board and the crew threw me a large rope knotted at the end that hung from somewhere high above. When I realized the rope was their only gangplank, I declined their invitation. They were gracious but sombre. Their sister ship, *Marques*, had recently sunk in the tall ships race from Bermuda to Halifax and some of their friends had died in that sinking. Port Hawkesbury was their first landfall since leaving Bermuda.

Captain John Adams and some of the crew were British. The young male sea cadets were Bermudian. There was an American from Rochester, New York, on board too. I offered to drive them to the store for supplies. The cooks accepted and we drove to the mall where they bought warm socks and cooking supplies. On our way back to the ship, I showed them where I lived and again offered my help should they need it. That afternoon the captain, the cooks and two pretty British girls knocked at my door and asked to use the phone. We chatted over milk and cookies. I wished them a safe journey and they left.

The next morning the ship sailed away from the wharf. Once offshore they raised some sails and headed up the Strait for the Canso Canal. I followed by car, hoping to see them all again at the Canal but no sooner had I parked the car when I heard a loud crack. The crew had attempted to take the ship through the Canal under sail and it hit the concrete canal and damaged the bowsprit. Their journey had to be postponed.

After they tied *Inca* by the canal office, I again offered to drive the captain back to Port Hawkesbury for repair supplies for this 138-year-old wooden ship. He confided that the ship's operating budget was very small. On the return trip, he remarked on the beauty of the rose window in St. David's Church on the hill above the Causeway.

The ship stayed in Port Hastings several days making repairs. My last sight of *Inca* was the day it left, under full sail, to continue its journey to the Great Lakes. *Inca*'s Canadian story had just begun.
—Marilyn MacPhee

In September 1992, *Crown Monarch* made history on two counts: by being the largest cruise ship to sail through the Canso Canal and the largest to stop for passengers at the Canal. The vessel was on a voyage from Alexandria, Vermont, to Quebec City, but ten minutes after the ship left dock in Halifax, it came to the attention of the crew that several passengers had not made it back to the ship on time and were stranded on a tour bus somewhere between the dock and Chester Basin. Once the oversight was recognized, the passengers were hustled onto a bus and driven to the Canal, where 41 sleepy passengers joined 474 others on their cruise ship at three in the morning.

For several years Anne Cormier, a resident of Port Hawkesbury, worked in a daycare facility, and she was used to dealing with excited children. However, the bus ride she took as chaperone to a group of band students on a day trip to Halifax proved to be a real test of her ability to keep them calm.

## "A CROSSING I'LL NEVER FORGET"

Wednesday, November 7, 2001, began as an ordinary day. Wisps of smoke curled from the chimney tops up through the crisp autumn air. It was the type of day that made me glad to be alive, a beautiful fall day.

*A transport truck overturned in a November 2001 storm.*

As my eleven-year-old son and I left home, my husband reminded me to take the cell phone, "Just in case; you may need it." Only later would I realize how important it would become. Our bus left Tamarac Education Centre in Port Hawkesbury a bit behind schedule due to a slight mechanical problem, but still in time to make it to the city on schedule. A school band trip to the city of Halifax, a three-and-one-half hour drive to see a concert, visit a museum and do a bit of shopping, offered too much excitement to the sixty grades five to eight students on the bus. A great cheer arose from the group as the bus began to move. This boisterous group was certainly geared to chatter and sing. Several children sang different songs and this led to a competition to see which half of the bus could sing louder than the other. Shortly after our departure, one of the parents commented, "I hope we get back before the big storm hits."

"Storm?" I thought, "Sure doesn't look much like a storm."

We arrived for the scheduled concert at the Rebecca Cohn Auditorium in Halifax with sixty wound-up kids. The concert by the Howard Cable and Stadacona Band was a smashing success and seemed to raise the kids' level of excitement, which one wouldn't think could have been possible. They wanted to be on the move again.

We left the Cohn after the concert for our next stop, the Museum of Natural History with all of its exciting displays. A light rain was falling but nothing indicated we should postpone any of our plans and hurry home. After our museum adventure we noted there had been a substantial drop in temperature. The rain had changed to snow. Everything was turning into a winter wonderland.

With the snow still falling and the children singing Christmas songs, we were soon homeward bound. The kids chattered excitedly and sang "Let it Snow." About twenty minutes out of the city the snow turned to rain again and I breathed a sigh of relief. An hour later we faced major gusts of wind and driving rain, but we still didn't have to worry. We were making great time despite the weather.

Near Antigonish, darkness fell. By this point, the wind was so strong we could feel the bus shake. The rain fell in torrents. Great gusts of wind buffeted the big vehicle, as the bus grew quiet. Now the children weren't as anxious to sing their songs.

When we were about twenty minutes from the Causeway, my husband phoned to relay a news bulletin from the local radio station. A transport truck had overturned on the Causeway. We should expect delays. I said I'd call back when we reached the Causeway. "We'd better phone the school and inform the administration and parents of our situation," the band teacher suggested.

Soon we arrived at the Causeway and learned the overturned transport was the least of our worries. Far more alarming were the pieces of debris that the gale-force wind and pounding surf washed up along the road. In my many trips across this Causeway in all seasons, I had never seen anything quite like this. Huge boulders were scattered everywhere. The RCMP informed us we could probably expect at least a one-hour delay. Again, phone calls were made to the school and waiting parents to reassure them everyone was safe.

Eventually a snowplough cleared the debris off the roadway. We watched in utter amazement as the plough driver made seven trips back and forth. By now the children were tired, hungry, and restless. The adults were the same.

Soon a cheer arose. Ever so slowly, a few cars began to move. But from our vantage point, we watched as the enormous waves washed over each vehicle. Some of the children were close to tears. "Will we be washed over the side?" a child close to me asked quietly. "Oh no," I replied, "Remember we are in a big bus and seeing our bus is larger and higher than the cars, the waves won't bother us. It'll be like going through a car wash."

With a slight nod and a quiet "okay," the child settled back in her seat.

It was dark, pitch black in fact, as we inched our way forward. There wasn't a sound in the bus. Everyone seemed to be holding their breath. Since there was no power, our only light came from the headlights. The bus driver exercised his many years of experience as he manoeuvred the large vehicle along, amid the blackness, boulders and debris. Suddenly there was a loud crunching sound: we hit a hole as large as a crater and the bus descended into it. We hit the surrounding debris, then—bang! An enormous wall of water hit our bus with such force the emergency hatch on the roof of the bus blew open. Water poured in. Frightened youngsters screamed. Thankfully, one chaperone, seated in close proximity to the open hatch, jumped into action and wrestled against the forces of the wind and rain to close the hatch. No more water poured in. So much for my silly "car wash" pretence!

Partway across, I looked out. To my horror, we were approaching a light standard. It was bent at an acute angle and swaying precariously in the gale. "Dear Lord, don't let that thing fall," I prayed as we slowly moved closer. I breathed a great sigh of relief when we were finally past. That trip over the dark, windy Causeway seemed to take an eternity. "Look, Mrs. Cormier," one of the kids said in the most welcome statement I'd heard all night. "It's the sign—'Welcome to Cape Breton'!" A great cheer arose simultaneously from both kids and adults on that bus. We had made it! We were home at last!

As we drove through the dark, deserted streets to Tamarac School we were truly thankful that we were back safe and sound. One thing I think we all learned is never to take our link to the mainland for granted. Most of us did not realize until the following morning just how close we actually had come to losing our "link" that night. One would never imagine that the roadbed could erode to such a degree. The hole we had hit the previous night was not just a hole. It was, in fact, a washed-out section of road, extending to nearly the centre line, where the pavement, sand bed, gravel and larger stabilizing rocks had all washed away. The hole was actually a large opening or gap that had come close to completely severing part of the road. The damage was so extensive that it was deemed impassable for almost two days while road crews worked hurriedly to make repairs. The restoration project lasted several weeks. The Causeway had weathered many storms in the past, but never in its forty-seven years of existence had it been in such danger of destruction as it was that night. Will we ever forget that crossing? Certainly not!
—Anne Cormier

# CHAPTER 8

# ON THE LIGHTER SIDE

"A sister of the bard was on her death bed." With these words, another story begins in a Cape Breton kitchen. Mix this with a bit of satire and an outrageous story and the Kitchen Ceilidh (an informal storytelling and music event) is underway. Wit, humour, ghost tales and comebacks are all part of the evening's entertainment, and nothing pleases the islander more than a good laugh, especially at themselves. Over the years the Causeway has been the subject of many of these stories and laughs.

David G. Jones the author of "Cape Breton Cause-why," was born in Truro, but moved to Cape Breton as an infant. He grew up in Glace Bay and attended University of Kings College in Halifax. He now lives in Ottawa.

## "CAPE BRETON CAUSE-WHY (1)"

**SCENE:** A run-down corner store. Two girls chat in front, holding cones.

*MARY:* S'bridge.
*BETH:* S'not a bridge.
*MARY:* S'bridge. S'big bridge.
*BETH:* S'not a bridge. My teacher said so.
*MARY:* Oh yeah!? What's she know? She build bridges?
*BETH:* She been everywhere. She been to Halfax. 'N Angonish. 'N she took a vacation once ta tha Sunrise Trail. She tole me.
*MARY:* Yeah. OK. But whats she know bout bridges?
*BETH:* When she went up there she went over the Causeway. 'N she said it wan't a bridge like lotsa people say.
*MARY:* So what is it then?
*BETH:* My teacher Ms. McInnis says "It's a cause-way." Bridges got a "span" she said.
*MARY:* Spam! Yer teacher says bridges is made of spam? That's stupid.
*BETH:* Not "spam." "Span." Means it goes over the water. A causeway goes through the water. That's what she says.
*MARY:* My uncle George got a bridge.
*BETH:* Yeah so what. Lotsa people got bridges. Where's his go?

*S'not a bridge, s'a causeway.*

MARY: Right in his mouth, Dear, right in his mouth (ha, ha).

BETH: You don't know nothin. Y'know that. You don't know nothin.

MARY: I say it's a bridge just like that bridge they built to Pee-e-eye.

BETH: S'not a bridge either.

MARY: E-l-i-z-a-b-e-t-h. That one goes over tha water!

BETH: That one's a "fixed link"—my teacher says. They call it a "flink."

MARY: So do they make flinks from spam too? (ha, ha, ha)

BETH: Teacher says the reason you are not getting ahead Mary Louise is because you are what she calls "cynical." And because you are "cynical," Mary Louise, maybe you otta get the flink outta here and leave us alone.

MARY: That suits me fine Lizzie Bee. Cause I'm gonna cross the Causeway. I'm gonna walk on the water just like that Causeway does. Just like Jesus Christ, Beth. Yep. I'm gonna walk on water, right up there and tell them what I think. I don't care whether it's a flink, a causeway, or a bridge. It's my way outta here Beth baby. And I'm takin it.

## "CAPE BRETON CAUSE-WHY (2)"

ALBERT: There's somethin I don't understand bye.

ED: Yeah? What's that Albert.

ALBERT: I don't understand, how come they got everything in Halifax, and we got nothin.

ED: That's easy. Cause. Just cause, that's why.

ALBERT: Yeah? Well how come when our kids get outta school they gotta go away. How come?

ED: Just cause, that's why.

ALBERT: 'Zat right? Well then how come we got all these politicans. And we got all these, like, "agencies" that are supposed to, you know, like balance things out.

ED: It's because, Albert, you know that.

ALBERT: Well I spose I do. But I wonder why, like everyone here just puts up with it. You know. Like nobody ever complains.

ED: Well Albert, it's like this. Cause it don't do you no good to complain anyway. Cause nobody's listenin'. That's cause why. That's why we got the "cause why" between here and the mainland.

—David G. Jones

For years David Harley, taking on the persona of General John Cabot Trail, the leader of a fictitious throng of rowdy party-goers known as the Cape Breton Liberation Army, has entertained audiences with his humorous slant on Maritime politics, sports and everyday life. After each performance, he ended his monologue with the now famous words, "Down with the causeway!" In response to such a suggestion, Hilton McCully, a retired teacher and author of "Fun Stories of the 90s," has written the following letter.

# AN RATHAD O'N-T-EILEANN (THE ROAD FROM THE ISLAND)

*GENERAL, SIR,*
I have listened to your treatment of various news items and wish to comment briefly.

It appears that you are trying to turn all newsworthy items to your advantage, Sir, in your obsession to destroy the causeway. This causeway is the only link which prevents the pretty island from drifting out into the western ocean, a derelict to be claimed by an ocean-going salvor, equipped for towing a pile of slag and millions of gallons of heavy water, the latter product being located at the Bay, b'y. Consider too, if you will, the loss of thousands of kilts, proscribed yearly by Environment Canada, August one to June thirty.

Now, Sir, before further effort on your part to destroy the causeway, you should think of certain benefits, accruing to your country, via the causeway.

I am sure you are aware that, recently, Angus MacAskill was transported from Halifax to St. Ann's. Would you destroy the one road to which he has access to visit the Mainlanders? There are also those sons and daughters who labour in the Common House in Ottawa. Would you sever this one link, by which they may return to Gleann and Beinn, with-

out an addition to some local airstrip?

Have you talked over your plan with the Barra MacNeills, the Door Knobs, John Allie, Rita MacNeil, and the Cape Breton Symphony? How would the Iona Connection ever connect with the mainland without the causeway? By the Bochan Bridge perhaps?

Where are Dan and Angus today? Are they down on the Mira, wondering about your crazy plan? Won't they be worrying about getting the Men of the Pits out of the deeps and into the Metro Centre for one more big "do" before the causeway is plastered all over Kelly's Mountain and the shores of Bras d'Or?

Recently I dreamed of a plan, hatched in the Cape Breton Highlands, a plan to move the budworms to the mainland. In my dream, I saw five hundred be-tartaned, pipe-bearing lassies. Each lassie wore a sprig of heather, and from her girdle there trailed a six-foot by two-inch strip of Cape Breton tartan. To the end of each strip of tartan was attached a freshly cut spruce bough. As the pipes struck up their skirling, whining dirge, an rathad O'N-t-Eileann, the lassies marched out of Port Hastings. As the sound of the lament hit the highlands, the budworms began to move out of the trees, down gleann and beinn, to the Canso crossing.

Now, Sir, if the causeway is blown up by your nefarious efforts, you risk leaving five hundred Cape Breton lassies stranded on the mainland. Also, delivery of unemployment cheques would be impeded. Worst of all, Bud the worm could be stranded on your side of the Strait.

It has been my experience that one should keep silent about a plan such as yours. Leave it to the Department of Transport. If you do this, I can assure you that in thirty or forty years, Canso tides will wash away this abominable link with the mainland. Patience is a virtue and virtue has its own reward.

General, Sir, please give these ideas of mine your careful consideration. Whilst you cogitate on these matters, would you let me have your considered opinion as to whether virtue virtually does have its own reward? I'll be in touch with you when I dream again.

*Slainnte mo charaid.*—Hilton McCully

David McClafferty was born in Annapolis Royal, and moved to Halifax at the age of 24. He retired from the CBC in 1996, having worked there as a technician for over 30 years. His wife believes he has a story for every occasion and about every place he's travelled, including a storm-stayed trip to Cape Breton.

## "THEY CAME ON ALL FOURS!"

While David was on a work assignment with a CBC mobile television unit he was storm-stayed at a motel in Port Hawkesbury along with many people who had just crossed the Causeway. Since this included the passengers from an Acadian Lines bus, the motel was filled. David said a man came in and asked for a room and was told there were none left. He said even a cot in the hall for him and his wife would be appreciated, otherwise they would have to sleep in the car. The desk clerk agreed and asked the man which way he came. He answered that they had come across the Causeway. The desk clerk said "That's impossible! The Causeway has been closed for hours!"

The man said, "Look outside!" Outside the man's wife was un-harnessing some dogs. They had harnessed the dogs to the front of the station wagon and his wife sat on the hood wearing goggles and directed him as he steered the car, which the dogs were pulling. The desk clerk told him they wouldn't be able to accommodate the dogs. The man said, "That's no problem they're sled dogs. They would rather sleep out in the snow." —David McClafferty

On his website, Cape Breton performer and entertainer Adam Cooke asks, "How does a 'one-man show' grab you?" Adam has developed an upbeat act that combines his interests in Maritime traditional music, singing, song-writing, comedy and satire. Perhaps one of his most interesting acts was played to the smallest audience on the Cape Breton Causeway.

## "CRUISING THROUGH THE CANAL"

The first week of July 2001 saw an American cruise ship pull into the Strait Area. Travellers on the *Cape May Light*, whose head offices are located in "The Boston States" (Massachussetts, to be exact), would receive a true taste of Cape Breton culture when it arrived in Port Hawkesbury on that fateful day. I was one of a gaggle of performers from Richmond and Inverness counties that would offer a sampling of the Island's many cultures—Scottish, Irish, French and beyond—in a pair of one-hour performances in the ship's main banquet hall.

It was an affair to remember. Arichat's Delores Boudreau, the Evangeline to my Gabriel, joined me for the Acadian portion of the program; mercifully, she would handle the dancing portion of our musical contribution. Long-time Port Hawkesbury highland dancing instructor Dale Ryan prepared another bit of light-on-our-feet entertainment, while bagpiper Wally Ellison and vocalist/MC/organizer Patrick Lamey were both resplendent in highland regalia. Veteran Richmond County fiddler Clif-

ford (Ciffie) Carter and sweet-voiced Heather Richards of Port Hawkesbury rounded out our crew. We came, we saw, we sang, we danced, we gave them a brief Gaelic lesson; in short, we had them in the palm of our hands.

We didn't, however, get paid right away. The cruise director, Jason, told Patrick that a head office mix-up had prevented a cheque from being readily available, but he promised to have it mailed to us as quickly as possible. (This would prove to be the least of the cruise line's problems, as it went bankrupt a mere five months later. Let the records show that there is no conclusive proof that Cape Breton music was responsible for the downfall of the *Cape May Light*.)

Later that evening, at the suggestion of Delores, we went through the drive-through window of the local Dairy Queen outlet and then took our ice cream treats to the Causeway to enjoy the ship's passage through the Canso Canal en route to Prince Edward Island. As the *Cape May Light* made its approach towards the swing bridge, the temptation proved too great for Patrick and me to resist, and we made our way towards the edge of the Canal to wave to the ship's passengers and crew. Who should appear on the main deck but Jason, our apologetic but friendly cruise director. "JASON!" Patrick called out, adding a friendly wave. "Hey, Pat," Jason responded with a smile. Then, much to my amazement, the normally staid Patrick Lamey bellowed in a voice loud enough to be heard by everyone on the Causeway and on the ship: "SEND US THE CHECK!" The smile on Jason's face became a bit pasty, eventually disintegrating into a grimace. I quickly realized the cultural absurdity of the situation: a gentleman in full Scottish regalia, kilt and all, demanding his money from an American, in the presence of a shocked Acadian, decked out in black vest and bright red sash. For the record, we got our check, only a few weeks later. But those on the *Cape May Light* and the Canso Canal got a visual image that may well rival any sight that has ever graced the Canso Causeway. —Adam Cooke

## "RINGING IN THE NEW MILLENNIUM"

I had already determined that I was going to welcome the year 2000 with two borderline-insane activities: getting a Mohawk haircut on December 31, and going for a polar bear swim in the frigid waters of Point Michaud Beach, just outside my homeland of L'Ardoise, Richmond County on January 1. However, as a newspaper reporter working and living in Port Hawkesbury, I knew there could be only one place to officially welcome the third millennium as it arrived in the Maritimes at midnight, Atlantic Standard Time. The Canso Causeway, of course—that symbol of great pain and great joy that has become an inextricable part of the Cape Breton experience. Oddly enough, nobody else attending a house party in nearby Port Hastings was chomping at the bit to join me at the Canso Canal on this frigid December night, which is particularly unusual when one considers that most of these revellers were actors with Under the Map Theatre. They've all been known to partake in strange activities onstage and off.

Finally, at ten minutes to midnight, I coaxed a petite blonde woman named Verna Bartlett to make the two-minute trek to the Causeway. Perhaps Verna, a professional karaoke coordinator who had just made her Under the Map acting debut, had an adventurous streak that the others lacked. Or perhaps she felt there were better ways to welcome 2000 AD than watching CMT's "Top 100 Country Videos of the Millennium."

We arrived at the Cape Breton side of the canal and unfurled a large Nova Scotia flag. A light breeze caught the provincial emblem as we counted down the final ten seconds of the twentieth century, before letting loose in a frenzy of cardboard-and-plastic-horn tooting. And then—because no single act could have been more appropriate for the

location—Verna and I sang Kenzie Mac-Neil's "The Island." About half a dozen drivers gaily honked their horns as they criss-crossed the cursed link and caught a glimpse of us on the island side. We followed the poignant lyrics of our Cape Breton anthem—"We'll follow the foot-steps of those on their way, and still ask for the right to leave or to stay"—with the French and English renditions of "O Canada." Coming into the last lines of the English version, I was overcome with emotion as I realized that this beautiful country had survived every separatist threat that had arisen over the previous three decades. We had outlasted the FLQ, Levesque, the Meech Lake and Char-lottetown accords, Parizeau, Bouchard, and two sovereignty referendums, in-cluding the 1995 nail-biter. Canada was still Canada in 2000. And the Causeway was still the Causeway, and Cape Bret-on was still Cape Breton. Because Cape Breton will ALWAYS be Cape Breton.
—Adam Cooke

"The Causeway is, in fact, a voyage of the heart for many, and the mere sight of it can cause even the strongest man to weep, and the weakest and battered woman to regain her faith in life. It is where the heart makes its decision to survive, to forgive, to move on or, inevitably in spirit or in body, to come home."

Erin Moore, former resident of Cape Breton

# CHAPTER 9

# WELCOME TO CAPE BRETON

Although many Cape Bretoners will argue that it was Canada that joined Cape Breton in 1955, in reality, large numbers of island dwellers had by that time left the island and joined the rest of Canada. Although some new industries have come to the island, providing work for its residents, a significant number of people have left, often not because they wanted to, but because they needed to in order to find employment. However, in interview after interview these same people say that the island holds a special place in their hearts and the Causeway, particularly the words "Welcome to Cape Breton" posted over the swing bridge, is the symbol of a true and deep-felt sentiment.

Catherine Kennedy, formerly from Port Hastings but now living in Bermuda, writes: "For many years, I took the existence of the Canso Causeway as proof that Cape Breton was special. It was no accident, I thought, that you had to pay to get onto the island, but you could leave for free whenever you desired, as if Cape Breton were a form of entertainment." Not only did the Causeway link local traffic

and former island residents as they returned home, it brought tourists to the Island. In 1958, when the Causeway was still considered a novelty, Iris and Frank Hayes decided Cape Breton would make an ideal destination for their honeymoon—but although the Causeway has been known to weave its charm on young love, on this journey it had an unusual way of making sure the trip was unforgettable. Here Frank and Iris tell how their first crossing as a married couple tested their relationship.

## "THE CAUSEWAY TESTS THE VOWS"

My husband, Frank, and I were married on July 5, 1958, in the United Baptist Church in Port Hilford, Guysborough County. We had decided that our honeymoon would take us across the new Causeway and around the beautiful Cabot Trail.

Following a delightful reception at the home of my grandmother, the late

*Frank and Iris Hayes*

*The car that gave the Hayes a memorable honeymoon at the Causeway.*

Mrs. Della B. Kinley, we were sent off in a cloud of confetti by a group of laughing well-wishers. They had blocked up the rear axle of our 1951 Ford and decorated it with streamers, bows and tin cans—all the traditional tricks played on newly married couples.

As the young, starry-eyed bride and groom, our last thought was of how much air remained in our tires. Later, we had reason to believe someone from our "decorating committee" released some for us. We paid our toll at the Causeway and proceeded to cross. Just then, we sensed the unmistakable symptoms of a flat tire and were forced to stop smack dab in the middle of the Canso Causeway!

We got out, Frank in his new wedding suit and I in my lovely blue "going-away" outfit, the car still sporting pink and white streamers. The right front tire was ruined and far too hot to handle, so we simply had to wait for it to cool. Every passing vehicle, each car, truck and bus serenaded us with its horn. The traffic seemed endless. Finally, the tire cooled so that Frank could change it. Then we went in search of a service station to buy a replacement tire. It was late afternoon on a summer Saturday, but we finally found one. It was after dark when we located our first motel, with a sadly depleted honeymoon fund. Our planned five-day trip had been shortened to three, but together we had weathered our first taste

of adversity and had a wonderful time.
—Iris & Frank Hayes

Although Tom and Keri MacInnes, teachers in Bowmanville, Ontario, didn't have quite the same experience as the Hayeses when they crossed the Causeway, it did play an important role in their courtship and wedding plans.

## "LOVE ON THE ROCKS"

*Thomas MacInnis, just before he proposed at the Causeway.*

My name is Thomas Charles MacInnes and I have been living in exile ever since I crossed the Causeway going west to attend Ryerson Polytechnical Institute and find a job. And, like many Capers in exile, I have tried to return "home" as often as finances and time have permitted. Every time I cross under the "Welcome to Cape Breton" sign, I give a little cheer, a little whoop, because now I am back on Cape Breton Island and it automatically feels like I am home. The sign became a beacon I waited for the entire drive home from Ontario. It was, next to actually arriving home in Glace Bay, the single most important spot on the entire journey. In my will, I actually have it stated that I want my ashes to be scattered there. I also imagined that when it came time to propose marriage, it would be a very scenic as well as an emotionally important location to do it in.

As luck would have it, I met my future wife in 2000 in Ontario. We both knew almost immediately that we were the one for each other and that marriage was the likely outcome of our relationship. I spent most of the school year getting to know Keri's parents. However, my mother lives in Glace Bay and does not like to travel. Thus, she did not meet Keri until the summer of 2001. Even though Keri and I had long since discussed marriage, I told her that out of courtesy to my mother, I would not officially propose to her until they met in person. So, that summer, we travelled to Glace Bay and Keri and my mother finally met. They hit it off wonderfully and the wedding plans actually started to take shape.

In a weird twist of fate, we actually found the wedding locale, arranged the reception, got the license, hired entertainment for our guests (the Inspirational Singers from Whitney Pier), and ordered flowers, all before the engagement happened. My plan was for us to be engaged under the "Welcome to Cape Breton" sign, but because of certain scheduling conflicts I couldn't come up with a plausible excuse for going all the way to the Causeway. However, we had decided to honeymoon at the Silver Dart Lodge and tour the Cabot Trail. So, when it finally came time to visit the Silver Dart to check it out and book our room, I managed to trick Keri into going the extra distance on the pretence of finally having my picture taken in a spot that was so special to me. Keri seemed to think this was a reasonable request, so off we went.

It rained all the way to Baddeck! I was beginning to panic in the car because obviously I couldn't go forward with the picture-taking ruse if it was raining. However, as if by divine intervention, the rain stopped not too far from the Causeway and the plan was able to proceed as scheduled.

The photo with me standing under the sign with the ring box in my pocket was the picture I convinced Keri I wanted for my own sentimental reasons. After the photo was taken we walked back across the bridge and I proposed in the parking lot just to the left after the bridge. Keri cried. Then we went to Rita's Tea Room and the rest is history. We had a wonderful wedding and have lived happily ever after.
—Thomas & Keri MacInnes

There's a window in Catherine Kennedy's parents' house that's square and single-paned, so it framed the Causeway perfectly. Catherine particularly liked the night view.

## "A PORT HASTINGS GIRL'S CAUSEWAY"

My uncle Christopher worked in a little booth in the ceiling of the Causeway's swing bridge. He presided over the levers and buttons that open the bridge to allow marine traffic through the canal. Back then, the words "Canso Canal" were spelled out in white stones against a slanting hill at the foot of an odd little red and white lighthouse.

Kids would "ride" on the swing bridge as it opened. I'm sure it wasn't sanctioned by whichever government department oversaw the Causeway, but Uncle Christopher and his colleagues would be far too busy doing the button-and lever pushing to stop us. What a thrill it was to watch the centre lines on the paved bridge break away from those on the road. The bridge would swing wide, bells clanging and lights blinking. It was the next best thing to the annual appearance of the Bill Lynch Show and its Tilt-A-Whirl. Certainly the most exciting vessel I saw go through the canal was the Royal Yacht Britannia, with no less a personage than the Queen Mother aboard. I waved so hard at the figure in turquoise with the matching feathered hat that I felt an instant empathy for the endless waving that was all in a day's work for her.

It wasn't all good, though. I worried about bad weather forcing the closure of the Causeway. I feared the acute appendicitis that would necessitate an emergency trip to St. Martha's in Antigonish. It never came to pass, but bad weather always made my stomach knot up, no doubt from thinking of the consequences of not getting across.

Then there were the years when a Causeway token was the price of "escape." When I was not yet a teen, Port Hawkesbury didn't have a library, but Mulgrave did. The trip to the Mulgrave Branch of the Eastern Counties Regional Library necessitated a trip across the Causeway and one of those tokens to get back home. Thank goodness my mother, a teacher, championed reading and would take my sister and me there every week or two. I would stock up, especially in summer, so that I would not go insane with boredom at the "stupid cottage" or on the "dumb boat." Today, I still love reading at our peaceful place on the Bras d'Or.

After high school, I spent a summer working for the Port Hastings Historical Society. 1980 marked the twenty-fifth anniversary of the opening of the Causeway. We researched its construc-

tion (as I recall, at least one huge truck is down in the deep gathering barnacles) and helped with the festivities. Mary Campbell Jamieson, her colour high and proudly wearing her tartan, led a foot parade across the Causeway. There were pipers and dignitaries. It was a highlight in the work calendar that summer.

In later years, whenever I came home from university, I always looked forward to seeing the sweep of Creignish Mountain and the Causeway. It never failed to give me that rush of feeling called "almost home." When I see the Causeway today, I think of Uncle Christopher and of all those rides on the bridge. Chances are there isn't a Port Hastings girl around who hasn't tried it at least once.

It's been years since I've crossed the Causeway to enter Cape Breton (now we fly), but I hope that the words "Welcome to Cape Breton" still appear in bold white letters on the top edge of the swing bridge. Perhaps the words are faded; perhaps they're gone. But I know this: they are imprinted, like a verbal hug, on the minds of thousands of far-flung Cape Bretoners. That's because crossing the Causeway means coming home.
—Catherine Kennedy


Every once in a while there's a small, seemingly insignificant shared moment in time that keeps returning to your thoughts long after the incident has passed. Such was the case the night I met Rorrie MacIsaac.

From my seat by the window in a local restaurant I watched as the remaining traces of daylight were squeezed away by the approaching night. Like a famous sunset painting, a display of golden light from the evening sun lingered over the Canso Causeway. It hung there for several minutes, pausing briefly before tucking its warmth behind Porcupine Mountain. The formation of the clouds reminded me that fall would officially arrive in just a few days. I allowed my thoughts to wander as I waited for the waitress to bring me the evening menu.

Suddenly I was brought back to

Have you ever wondered who put the dent in the "Welcome to Cape Breton" sign? Mary Janet MacDonald has the answer: "A number of years ago my cousin Burke MacDonnell from Mabou was a young man driving a truck for his father. He was coming towards Cape Breton across the Causeway with his truck when a pole from the truck hit the bridge and to this day there is a big ding in the 'Welcome to Cape Breton' sign."

my present surroundings by the words spoken by a round-faced gentleman seated in the corner of the restaurant. His voice carried across the small room. "Forty years ago I crossed that causeway," he began. "I left family and friends and I never returned in all that time until two hours ago. When I came back across I could picture the day I left like it was yesterday. I remember that there were hundreds of fiddlers, pipers and dignitaries all around. It must have been the day it opened."

I couldn't help but overhear the words he spoke. I looked around to see whom he was addressing. It was then that I realized he was trying to engage in conversation with another guest seated at the next table. But this man was a reluctant participant. He kept shuffling his cutlery from side to side and poking at the food on his plate. It was obvious that he didn't want to talk.

I'm not certain if the round-faced gentleman noticed this mood or if he was just one of those few people who walk the earth, always able to look at the brighter side. In any case, he did not give up. Instead he continued to make remarks about the lovely evening and about how the little town had changed since he left forty years ago. Finally his persistence paid off.

"I can't agree with you. It isn't a nice evening," said the guest at the next table. "They can't even serve a hot steak around here. And yes, the weather's nice tonight, but it hasn't been. I can't wait to get back to Montreal."

With that remark, the conversation began in earnest and for a while I was just an eavesdropper, listening as the two businessmen and world travellers exchanged stories, switching from French to English as the conversation warranted. Before long the disgruntled traveller told his new friend that he thought he'd salvage what he could of the evening by finding the bar and getting drunk. My tell-tale smile gave away the fact that I had understood the words even though they had been spoken in French. At that point the round-faced gentleman drew me into the conversation.

"I see you understand French," he said as he lifted his coffee cup and made his way toward my table. "My name is Rorrie MacIsaac."

"Would you like to join me?" I asked as I motioned for him to take the chair opposite me. Rorrie needed no second invitation. Immediately he made himself comfortable and started to talk. No longer was he talking about business and world travel. Now the conversation centred on his homecoming, his Scottish heritage, and his love of Celtic music. He had never grown away from his roots and his love of the culture he remembered from his boyhood. He told me that his fiddle had always remained a close companion during his world travels.

Suddenly his mood changed, and he lowered his voice. Quietly he spoke of his love for his wife. She wasn't with him this evening. Earlier he'd mentioned that he was travelling on a spur of the moment whim from a northern community in Ontario. He had endured three long, hard days of driving, driving, driving, only stopping when the car needed gas or when he was too exhausted to continue.

Something was drawing him back. "Has his wife died?" I wondered to myself.

The conversation continued: oil business, computers, music, and family names, MacDonald, MacIsaac and Gillis. The restaurant emptied and filled again, but the talk flowed on and on. Finally, I asked him what he wanted to accomplish during his visit. Earlier in our conversation he told me that he hadn't kept in touch with his family on the island. In fact, he didn't know if any of them were still living here. He also mentioned that he had no set agenda, and as far as sightseeing was concerned, it didn't seem to matter what he saw. Yet it was obvious that he was being drawn back to this island and the home of his Scottish ancestors.

"I didn't think I'd tell my story to anyone," he said in answer to my question. "I have cancer and I came back to feel my roots, to get away from people who would look me in the eye and say, 'You look good; how do you feel?' I came to prove to myself that I could still drive and drive and drive. I finally made it. I've come home."

We talked some about his disease. Then we shook hands, offered each other our best wishes and took our different paths into the night. Ten years have passed since that meeting. I often wonder why I changed my plans and ate at that particular restaurant that night, instead of the one I usually visited down the road. I wonder if you beat cancer? I wonder if you were ever able to tell your friends how you really felt? I think of you, Rorrie MacIsaac, as a gentleman who looked death in the face and decided to live while you still had time. You enjoyed the sunset, you laughed at life and you followed your heart home.

## "MOVING ON"

When I think of Cape Breton, I realize the Celtic spirits have cast a spell on my heart. I'll admit it, when I first moved to the Island in 1974, the Causeway was my escape route. It led me back to the mainland, to cities and people and family. I was convinced the Causeway had brought me to the end of the earth and if someone argued that point, I'd counter with, "Maybe you're right, but if it's not the actual end, I'm sure you can see it from here." I realize now that I have developed an appreciation for the scenery, the culture, and the way of life away from the hustle and bustle of the cities, but I suspect the real reason for my affection goes much deeper.

Like many other young people of my generation, in the sixties it was necessary for us to leave our Maritime roots in order to gain work. But after living in "Upper Canada" for five years, my husband, Hugh, and I decided we wanted to bring our daughters, Heather and Heidi, back to the Maritimes, to be closer to our families and the Maritime way of life. The lifestyle suited us—knowing our neighbours, the sense of community and the beauty of our surroundings—so it

was with a heavy heart that, twenty-nine years later, I trudged up the hill towards our West Bay home. During the years I'd lived here, this walk by the lake had always been a time of renewal, but this day was different. Tomorrow I'd cross the Causeway to the mainland, and it would mark an end to my time in Cape Breton.

I have been back to the island several times since our move, and as we near the Causeway I feel as though I'm coming home. I note the white-capped waves and the jewelled patches of sunlight dancing on the water. A brisk wind blows spray over the Causeway as if to wash our car of its mainland soil. The Causeway has become the symbol of my ties to the Island.

Once home I find the treats from nature are still here; the pair of eagles still perch on the tree below our house; the moonlight still dances on the water and lights the trees that frame the edge of the beautiful Bras d'Or. Yes, there have been changes—around me I see growth, new buildings and dreams for the future. But the biggest reason I come back to the Island is to see the people. Here I can go into my friend's kitchen and pull up a chair, knowing my friend will take time to put on a cup of tea and make me feel welcome.

Each time I cross the Causeway and leave Cape Breton I realize part of me will never leave. I have just moved on.
—Elaine Ingalls Hogg